# *Mo' Dreamin'*
*Big Easy Dreamin' • Volume 2*

To Michael & Linda:

May your days be filled with Carnival glitter!

Enjoy the parade!

**Praise for *Big Easy Dreamin'* (Vol. 1)**

"A fast and loose read for those who know and love Sin City and those who want to get to know it better."
—Julie Whitehead, Spotlight On The Arts; *Jackson, Miss.*

". . . the author, quite comfortably and enjoyably, becomes part of the narrative—interested and interesting—on a fully leaded, high octane kick . . . clearly this book was a labor of love."
—Scott Naugle, Sun Herald; *Biloxi, Miss.*

"Great stuff! After you finish *Big Easy Dreamin'*, let me know if you want to go in on an apartment in New Orleans."
—Jill Conner Browne, *bestselling author of* The Sweet Potato Queens Book Of Love.

"JC's cooked up a flavorful gumbo. He takes so much unabashed pleasure in The City That Care Forgot, it's impossible not to get caught up in it."
—Julie Smith, *Edgar Award-winning author of* New Orleans Mourning *and* Mean Woman Blues.

"For those who aren't enthralled with the Crescent City, it must be because they haven't seen it through the author's eyes. Or seen his hauntingly appealing photos that accompany each essay in this made-to-fit-in-your-travel-bag book. *Big Easy Dreamin'* is just plain fun to read!"
—Susan O'Brien, Clarion-Ledger; *Jackson, Miss.*

# Mo' Dreamin'
## Big Easy Dreamin' • Volume 2

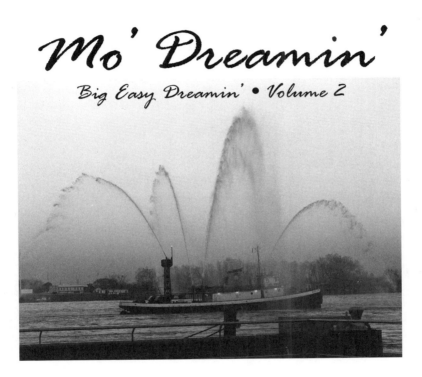

### By JC Patterson

sookie books
MADISON · MISSISSIPPI

Entire contents copyright © 2003 by JC Patterson
All rights reserved

ISBN 0-9741945-0-6

All photos by JC Patterson, unless noted.
Scans and enhancements by Bert Douglas.
Designed by Jason W. Moulder

First Edition

PRINTED IN THE UNITED STATES OF AMERICA

To Bert Douglas,

. . . my partner in crime; a consummate stage villain and hellacious photo fixer-upper. From my moans of discontent to my cries of victory, you listened, you counseled, and you cheered. This one's for you!

# Acknowledgements

Brenda & Sean Patterson; Sissy Leggett, Dae-Li Thompson; Shirley Ainsworth; Deborah Blakeney; Patricia Meek; John DeMarco; Pat Ogden; Sue Quiroz; Anne, Stan and Christopher Rice; Janis Petru; Tim Dorsey; Cindy Kelly; Ted O'Brien; Deb and Keith Wehmeier; Carson and Martha Lane; James Gandy; Theresa Watts; Janice Cartier; Amy Loewy; Bert Douglas; Jason Moulder; Wayni Terrell; John Connolly; Ritchie & Heather Champagne; New Orleans Preservation Resource Center; The Garden District Book Shop; Britton Trice; The Ritz Carlton-New Orleans; The Napoleon House; Lafitte's Blacksmith Shop; Marie Laveau's Voodoo Bar; Joey K's Restaurant; WWOZ, 90.7 FM; Carl Mack Presents; The Audubon Zoo; The Aquarium Of The Americas; IMAX Theatre; Blaine Kern's Mardi Gras World; The Children's Museum; Six Flags Over New Orleans; The New Orleans Spiritual Voodoo Temple; The Voodoo Museum; Words And Music, Inc.; The Tennessee Williams Literary Festival; French Quarter Festivals, Inc.; Krewe Of Muses; *Gambit Weekly*; *Mardi Gras* Magazine 2003; Musee Conti; *Offbeat* Magazine; The New Orleans Jazz & Heritage Festival; Krewe Of Barkus; Krewe du Vieux; The Mardi Gras Indian Council; and a big thanks to Kyle Jennings for the great lunch and literary insight.

# Contents

**Foreword** *Mardi Gras Dominoes*. . . . . . . . . . ix

## §1 *Friends*

Sissy's Balcony. . . . . . . . . . . . . 3
Aunt Shirley . . . . . . . . . . . . . . 7
The Lady Jester . . . . . . . . . . . . 13
Kindred Spirits . . . . . . . . . . . . 17
Suzie Q . . . . . . . . . . . . . . . . 23
Orange Crushin'. . . . . . . . . . . . 28
Cin's City . . . . . . . . . . . . . . . 33
Stan. . . . . . . . . . . . . . . . . . 37

## §2 *Customs*

Strut Your Mutt . . . . . . . . . . . . 45
Krewe With A Vieux . . . . . . . . . . 49
Braggin' In Brass . . . . . . . . . . . 53
Social Aid . . . . . . . . . . . . . . . 59
Injuns . . . . . . . . . . . . . . . . . 63
Satchmo In The Summer. . . . . . . . 67
Festivals Acadiens . . . . . . . . . . . 71
Make Mine Muses . . . . . . . . . . . 75

## §3 *Historical References*

| | |
|---|---|
| Wedding In Wax | 81 |
| Train-ing Day | 85 |
| Rollin' On The River | 89 |
| The Baroness | 93 |
| Hoodoo | 97 |
| Makin' Groceries | 105 |
| Street Talk | 109 |

## §4 *Dis 'n Dat*

| | |
|---|---|
| Kid Stuff | 117 |
| Uptown Rulers | 121 |
| WWOZ | 123 |
| Write Where You Live | 127 |
| Call For Distress | 131 |
| Time Well Spent | 135 |
| That Big Easy Feeling | 141 |

**Afterword** *Sin City Self Serve* . . . . . . . 144

**Sources** . . . . . . . . . . . . . . 146

**The Author** . . . . . . . . . . . . 147

# Foreword

## — Mardi Gras Dominoes —

I'M IN THE MIDST of a heavenly scenario. It's Mardi Gras morning, 10:15 AM on a Fat Tuesday. The sky is a gorgeous blue with just a hint of clouds passing over, as if to wink at the merriment below. The temperature is set at an invigorating 76 degrees. I'm sitting in my cherry red foldout chair in front of the Walgreens on the corner of Napoleon and Claiborne. A perfect spot to watch the parade.

Rex is turning the corner amid cheers and expectant, waving hands. I take a swig of my Abita Amber, a rush passes through me, and I begin to wave, too.

If this were a beer commercial, I would be center stage.

Beads begin to rain down on me; huge strands, shiny and long. I smile at the passing floats, marvel at their colorful creations. A masked rider spots me in the crowd and points in my direction. He rears his arm back and hurls a sack of multicolored beads straight at me. I rise and receive his gift (it nearly knocks me back down), then quickly stash it in the tote bag hanging alongside my chair.

A kid looks down longingly from the ladder next to me. He's dressed up like a clown (of course). I reach in my holding bag, pull out several strands of my prized catch and raise them up to his delighted surprise.

"Thanks, mister," he smiles. And so do I.

It's all about sharing, seeing the look on other people's faces as you turn over a smidgen of your faux treasure. Passing on the revelry like a row of purple, gold and green dominoes.

My heavenly scenario (as opposed to a purgatorial scenario, which is anywhere outside New Orleans) is replete with profound joy, laughter, costumed nuttiness, careless and creative themes emblazoned on tractor-pulled floats, and children's squeals as they dash back and forth from street to sidewalk, their arms crammed with plush toys. A true Carnival atmosphere.

Rex ruffles its colors like a giant peacock flexing wings. Marching bands, drill teams, cars packed with royalty, they all pass in formation, heading up Napoleon to St. Charles, hanging a left and continuing downtown to Canal, amid the million or so revelers ready to grab, cheer, drink and laugh.

Here is New Orleans at her finest, at her merriest. Joie de vivre transcendent. A memory I hang in my mind's Happy Place. The only thing missing is my son, who would've loved to have all those plush animals raining down like a Toys 'R' Us monsoon.

If you're familiar with my first volume of memories, interviews and New Orleans history, you know there's a lot more levels to the Crescent City than just parades and beads. I've met some wonderful people since the book came out. People who were touched by my tales and in turn, touched me with their unique stories. Once again, it's like those Mardi Gras dominoes: one brushes the other and on and on until there's a whole lot of good times filling the room.

After *Big Easy Dreamin'* hit the shelves, I realized there were so many more stories I had to tell; enough ingredients and tidbits to make a second flavorful gumbo. The book brought such happiness to so many people, I thought, why not spread a little more roux over the concoction.

So here it is, y'all. *Mo' Dreamin': Big Easy Dreamin', Volume 2*. Sample all you like. Have fun again.

And begin construction on your own heavenly scenario.

*"OK, I'm ready to pop the top, light a smoke, grab a pillow, and indulge myself into another delicious book of memory joggers . . . new and old tales . . . about a city that one could write a million stories on reflections and experiences. My advice? GET BUSY!!! NOW!!!"*

—Patricia Meek, after reading the Foreword
(the only thing I had written at the time)

*B. B. King parades with the Krewe of Zulu*

## §1 Friends

# Sissy's Balcony

IT WAS A LIFELONG fantasy. The privilege of having an apartment right in the middle of the French Quarter. A block and a half from Bourbon Street. A balcony to die for.

And every weekend for an entire year, two ladies called it party central.

Sissy and her roommate Dai-Le (from Daiona Leigh) live in Magnolia, Mississippi, just a spit from McComb. An easy hour and a half's drive to the Crescent City. Sissy's a dental assistant for her brother's practice in Magnolia; Dai-Le is a medical coder for Southwest Mississippi Regional Medical Center.

Sissy has loved New Orleans all her life. Her mother, Nan, had grown up along the River Road, and would take Sissy into town when she was a little girl to experience the big city.

Through persistence and a whole lot of luck, the second floor apartment in the six hundred block of St. Peter Street became their weekend residence. And a source of pleasure they'll always cherish.

"We had been looking for months," Sissy said. "Dai-Le and I were sitting in Royal Blend (a coffee house on Royal Street) and overheard two people talking about a place going on the market. With the perfect balcony." The couple, Babs (a tarot reader in Jackson Square) and Les (a musician), informed the inquisitive searchers about the current renters' planned exodus to Abita Springs, across Lake Pontchartrain in St. Tammany Parish. The decision was so fresh, the tenants hadn't even informed their landlord.

The apartment was only a couple blocks from where Sissy and Dai-Le were sitting.

"When I saw that balcony from the street, it really didn't matter how big the apartment was," said Sissy. "I didn't care if it was a broom closet. I wanted that balcony."

The Magnolia duo acquired the landlord's name and began calling in earnest once a week. They eventually signed a one year lease…from April to April.

If you've meandered down Rue St. Peter, the infamous lane that hooks up with The Crazy Corner bar on Bourbon, you've probably seen Sissy and Dai-Le's balcony. It's the balcony with a slight dip to it just down and across from The Gumbo Shop.

I've often wondered if the ancient balcony was on the verge of collapse. Since personally visiting, dodging raindrops, catching an impromptu wedding procession, and just enjoying the atmosphere of a N'awlins night, I can attest: that balcony's gonna hang around for years to come.

I met Sissy and Dai-Le on a cold, wet January afternoon in 2001. My friend Debra had gifted them a copy of *Big Easy Dreamin'* a few weeks earlier. Sissy had taken it into the bathroom to peruse a tale or two. She didn't come out 'til she'd read it cover to cover. You can't buy marketing like that.

When I heard about Sissy's pleasant reaction (and the location of their apartment), I had to drop by.

It was 4:00 PM on a soggy Saturday. An hour earlier, the bottom had dropped out over the streetcar I rode in from Uptown. My flimsy umbrella had all but turned inside out from persistent winds. Not a pleasant day to hawk my book to French Quarter merchants. Would this evening's Krewe du Vieux parade be a washout, too?

Well, that's another story…

The rains had just called an intermission when I phoned Sissy from Arcadian Books, just around the corner from their entrance. A couple minutes later, she stood in front of an ancient iron fence that led to her weekend digs. Suddenly, I didn't feel so alone and washed out.

Sissy is a vibrant, earthy looking woman in her mid-forties. Thin and taut, approaching five feet nine. Short, dark hair with grey streaks. A proud and content smile. An easy talker. Her son says she could have a conversation with a light pole.

We traversed down a long narrow walkway and up creaking wooden stairs to the entrance. Then I was acquainted with the magic.

The apartment is a small yet very open area with two bedrooms, tiny kitchen and bath, and a spacious living room that opens onto the famous balcony through twin windows. Eclectic and funky touches give their French Quarter "estate" the perfect atmosphere. A woman's mannequin torso bears the signatures of all their guests.

"Living in the Quarter gives you a whole different perspective," Sissy beams. "You see things from that balcony the tourists miss. Like the night people, the folks who come out late." Sissy and Dai-Le used the bucket-on-a-rope method to give and retrieve things to and from the street. "We might send down a candle or toilet paper to a needy street person. But no beer. They could get that anywhere."

They quickly made friends with the neighborhood. Gary lives directly across in the attic loft once occupied by Tennessee Williams. "He decorated our balcony for Christmas," said Dai-Le, an attractive, blue-eyed blonde in her mid-thirties. "Gary used to wake us up by shining a laser pointer from his loft into our living room," Sissy laughs.

Other new acquaintances included Babs and Les, the couple who'd paved the way; Mercedes, a bartender in the Sazerac bar at the Fairmont Hotel; Winky Fontaine, an artist in Jackson Square; Lee, a musician who turned them on to the best po-boys and sno-balls around, and woke them with his distinctive bird whistle; Smiley, the balloon artist, who shot balloons into their window from street level; and the crowd at Oz.

Around the corner on Bourbon, one of the more colorful gay bars, Oz, offers Drag Bingo three nights a week. Hosted by drag queen Bianca Del Rio, the bingo parlor fills up quickly Thursday and Fridays from 6-8 and Sundays 5-7. "It's a blast," laughs Sissy. "You've got to experience it."

She kept a journal, though not as thorough as Sissy would've liked. Entries include discovering neighborhood eateries the tourists never frequented, their first New Orleans spring, French Quarter Fest, Jazz Fest, the Southern Decadence Parade, Halloween, Christmas, New Years…right up to Mardi Gras. Plus the constant parade of weekend guests stretched out on the living room floor.

One of Sissy's fondest memories was celebrating her son Andy's engagement. "This left hand appeared in the door with a diamond ring on it."

Then there was the view from their balcony.

"I was blissfully happy watching, not interacting," said Sissy. "It's a free show that changes every minute."

Sissy and Dai-Le still make regular pilgrimages to Sin City. There are plenty of Quarter friends to stay with. But they sure miss their balcony.

"My son really put things in perspective one night when we were all sitting around," said Sissy. "He looked at me, smiled and said, "Nan (Sissy's mom) would've loved this."

# Aunt Shirley

SHE WAS ALWAYS the goodwill ambassador to Carnival. One week a year, her spacious, two-story house on a quiet backstreet in Gretna was filled to the brim with scores of visitors who'd come to party. Her army-sized servings of gumbo and spaghetti were legendary and tasted better than any restaurant. From her eclectic table decorations to her authentic glass Carnival beads, to the mindset she bestowed on everyone she touched, this lady encompassed the spirit of Mardi Gras like no one else I've met.

Shirley Ainsworth (Aunt Shirley to the world) is like a precious Carnival artifact freefloating in her own one-woman museum. A constant smile empowers her sixty-plus years in a compact five-foot-two-inch frame. Blonde hair in a tight perm to match her light framed glasses. Inquisitive blue eyes that seem to ask, "Does everyone have a place to sleep?" or "Can I refill your plate?"

Everyone liked going to Aunt Shirley's. Especially when she moved from her tiny home in Marrero into her son's 2,500 square foot estate a few miles east in Gretna in the Terrytown area. We're talking the West Bank, across the Mississippi River from New Orleans proper. Cross the bridge dubbed the Crescent City Connection and you're in Gretna. Keep going west and you end up in all those small communities like Harvey, Marrero, Westwego, Bridge City, Avondale, and Waggaman.

The West Bank has its own Mardi Gras parades. They're smaller, less flashy and more economical. Perfect for the kids. Many of

Shirley's visitors chose to stay and catch the West Bank parades like King Arthur, NOMTOK (New Orleans Most Talked-of Krewe), Poseidon, Grella, Ulysses, Adonis, and Alla (short for Algiers, Louisiana)—the fourth oldest parading group, that began back in 1933. Another great advantage to staying on the West Bank is being able to park near the ferry launch at Algiers Point, catch the free ferry ride over to the Riverwalk, and saunter down to wait for Endymion. When the parade's over, you take your stash of beads and cups back to the ferry and avoid the traffic.

And we'd always bring the best catch back for Shirley. That was the unspoken house rule. Shirley would then display your beads for all to see.

She never accepted donations. I tried several times to pitch in for the electric bill, but Aunt Shirley refused. That's just how she is.

I met Shirley Ainsworth through a mutual friend of mine and Brenda's: a real relative, mind you. Deborah Blakeney hails from Taylorsville, Mississippi, but she's lived and worked in Jackson for nearly twenty years. Deborah's a cardiac nurse at Baptist Hospital and Shirley's her real aunt. "Going to New Orleans was always a big deal to me as a little country bumpkin, and Aunt Shirley always made it special," Deborah reminisced. "She always had room for any and everyone who wanted to stay and she always had food. Shirley's the most nonjudgmental person I have in my family. I'd like to think I got that trait in some way."

It was a few short weeks before Mardi Gras 1995. I was looking for a place to stay, in lieu of all the overpriced hotel rooms. Deborah and her roommate Shelley informed me about this nice lady they were descending upon: Deborah's Aunt Shirley. "She's got plenty of room," Deborah said. "Just bring a sleeping bag." To my delight, my next four Carnivals were staged at Shirley Central.

Shirley shared her son's house for seven years with a pug named Barkley, several noisy canaries, fabulous doll and thimble collections, and Victor, a compact Guatemalan, who divided the rent and did maintenance for a nearby middle school.

Victor never failed to surrender his room to Mardi Gras visitors, often camping out on the living room floor on a small pallet. Whenever I occupied this quiet gentleman's humble bed, I made sure to thank him profusely. I still recall all of Victor's soccer memorabilia that hung on his walls and lined the dresser and shelves. I felt like

I'd disturbed the delicate balance this impoverished immigrant had solidified within the minute confines of his space.

"Oh, Victor don't mind," remarked Shirley, in her light Cajun accent. "Enjoy your visit."

Shirley resided in the New Orleans area for forty-eight years; thirty-seven of them in Marrero. The oldest of seven children, she was raised in the small pine belt community of Center Ridge in Smith County, Mississippi. She attended Draughn's Business College in Jackson, where Shirley met her future husband. Clarence Rodriquez was a Louisiana boy; his father was Spanish and his mother Cajun French. With close family ties to the Bayou State, the couple moved to the New Orleans area in 1953.

"I raised two sons and three daughters on Francis Street in Marrero," Shirley said. The family lived a half block from the Mardi Gras parade route. "Everybody would come by," Shirley recalled. "We always had people coming in."

Shirley was married three times. "I had three kids with the first husband and two with second." Shirley's first marriage ended after twelve years. Her n° 2, Dominique Vicari, was a popular deputy in Jefferson Parish. They were wed sixteen years. Her third marriage to Carlos Soto lasted twelve years. "The first two passed away; I don't want to talk about number three."

After divorcing Soto, Shirley took back her maiden name. And a boarder. Victor was a "good young man," according to the priest at St. Theresa's. He just needed a place to stay. That arrangement lasted sixteen years. "I could tell you stories about Victor's turbulent childhood in Guatemala," Shirley confided. "He's like an adopted son to me."

In 1993, Shirley was awarded a marvelous opportunity. One of her sons, a merchant seaman, offered the long-time Marrero resident a chance to live in a much larger house he had purchased in Gretna. She immediately accepted. Victor and Barkley came, too.

For seven years, Shirley was the lady of the manor, opening up her new digs to Carnival carousers eager for a place to crash. "Come on down, bring your sleeping bag," she'd say. "This is bed, but not bed and breakfast." Even Shirley's mother, "a Mardi Gras hound dog," according to her daughter, was often escorted in from Center Ridge, Mississippi. Sons, daughters, grandkids, nieces, nephews, and folks she'd never met (like me) filled every room, every hallway

and breakfast nook, poring over Shirley's *Times-Picayune*, eager to read about the day's festivities

In the fall of 1999, Aunt Shirley received the bad news. Her son had a good financial opportunity to sell the house. Shirley had to move. In her mid-sixties and on a fixed income, she wouldn't readily be able to live just anywhere. Shirley's closest family was two hours away in Hattiesburg, far from the area she'd made a home for nearly half a century. On January 8, 2000, Shirley headed for the Hub City.

"People started calling me a few weeks before Mardi Gras," Shirley recalled. "They'd say, 'Where are you? I'm so mad. I wanted to make reservations.'"

"I was mad at myself, but I had a decision to make," she said.

Shirley was reluctant to return to the pine trees of her youth; she was admittedly hostile. "The move was taking me out of my world," she recalled. Within a few weeks, Shirley and her sister Beverly found a quaint three bedroom dwelling on the outskirts of Hattiesburg.

"Two bedrooms and a doll room," corrects Shirley.

Victor remained in New Orleans. Barkley had to be put to sleep at fourteen years after developing emphysema. Shirley still has a couple canaries chirping about. Her sister Beverly and several grandchildren occupy her time. "I'm still happy," she smiled. "It's just different."

We miss the gracious lady who had to abandon her Mardi Gras ship at the start of the new millennium. I still keep in touch with Christmas cards and an occasional call. It's good to hear her voice. Aunt Shirley provided dozens of revelers with happy memories of a Carnival roof over our heads, a plate of gumbo on the table and an everpresent smile from our very own Carnival Queen.

"She told me when she dies, she wants a jazz band to play at her funeral," said niece Deborah.

No one deserves it more.

# The Lady Jester

CARSON AND MARTHA LANE have been spreading the Big Easy spirit for over ten years…from heights of up to ten thousand feet. When flying low, beads are flung from the heavens to outstretched hands. Purple, gold and green stripes glint off the sunlight; ribbons whip in the wind. Mardi Gras music cascades throughout the field below, heralding the passing of The Lady Jester.

Pilot Carson sports a neat, white beard with matching hat and theme T-shirt. His smiling eyes give away a spunkiness that belies his quiet demeanor. But in the air, Lane is all business. If you're a rider, you don't ask questions, you don't give advice. You enjoy the silence and the landscape, awaiting Carson's next order.

Martha's the social chairperson for the duo, the jester-queen. One usually hears her before spotting the shoulder-length dark hair, the kind eyes and the gold glitter outlining her purple T-shirt knotted at the waist. Martha is all grins and excitement, offering hugs and a strand of beads to fellow balloonists in town for competition. "Carson's cookin' up jambalaya for lunch," she proclaims.

The Baton Rouge couple never thought retirement would be so much work. Or so much fun. Carson was a mechanical engineer for over thirty years. His attention to detail was a natural transition to pilot and balloon keeper. Martha was involved as a marketing consultant and a featured speaker at conventions. They'd both been considering the ballooning life since Baton Rouge is a strong area for the sport. Over thirty teams operate in and around Louisiana's state capitol.

When the U.S. National Balloon Championships came to Louisiana in 1989, the Lanes had the privilege of officiating. They never looked back. "We purchased our first balloon from an individual in early 1990," said Carson. Later that year, the Lanes nailed down a solid theme and the balloon that would define them: The Mardi Gras Magic. "We wanted our theme to celebrate the spirit of Mardi Gras," said Martha. "Our motto says it all: Everyday is (Fat) Tuesday."

I first caught sight of The Mardi Gras Magic over Labor Day weekend, 1993. Jackson was hosting its first-ever Sky Parade at the airport and balloonists were out in full force. Even though a hundred or so hot air balloons flew that weekend, the purple, gold and green colors of the Mardi Gras Magic drew me like a magnet. The Carnival music playing from the van's speakers and the crew with their "natural party environment," as Martha calls it, made me want to hang around. Crew members wore white T-shirts with a colorful rendering of the MGM and the slogan: The Most Celebrated Balloon in Louisiana.

Martha handed me a trading card with The MGM's photo and credentials printed proudly on both sides. I walked away from the balloon field with a big smile on my face.

Brenda and I had crewed in Canton a couple months earlier during the Mississippi Championship Hot Air Balloon Festival fourth of July weekend. We'd been crammed in with a very stuffy family who treated us like hired help. After leaving the Lanes and their entourage, I knew who I wanted to crew with next time.

I called Carson and Martha in Baton Rouge a few weeks prior to the Canton race in '95. It didn't take much to convince them that my wife and I were that little lagniappe they needed to complete their crew.

Over the next five years, Brenda and I got to experience ballooning from a New Orleans perspective. It was a lot of work: looking for the right takeoff location, hauling out the basket, balloon and fan, then holding on to that big sucker while it filled up and rose into the sky. Then you'd say a silent prayer that the pilot would point at you at the last possible second to hop in the basket and ascend with him into the heavens.

Carson invited the two of us to fly with him on two occasions near sunset. Wow, what a view! What a romantic high. Brenda kissed me gently at a thousand feet over sprawling cotton fields while Carson turned on the propane burner to keep us afloat. It didn't matter where you landed: a cow field with angry heifers, in six foot tall grass with unseen briars that ripped at your legs, or a neighbor's backyard; there was always a party when the work was done. Champagne was poured over the "virgin" flyers with Mardi Gras music playing in the background. And the Balloonists Prayer is said aloud:

> "The Winds have welcomed you with softness.
> The Sun has blessed you with its warm hands.
> You have flown so high and so well,
> That God has joined you in your laughter,
> And He has set you gently back again
> Into the loving arms of Mother Earth."

And then there were two. The Lady Jester first inflated in the Superdome in 1996 at the Kids Fair. She first flew in Canton that same year with Martha, Teresa "T" Watts and Carson on board. T, Brenda and myself, along with Jacksonian James Gandy were the Canton coalition for three years. Let the good time roll!

Carson and Martha have competed in local, state, regional and national competitions. Fiesta in Albuquerque is the most magnificent venue with over 1,000 balloons represented. "We've won some, came in second in some, but had fun at all the competitions," said Martha.

The Lanes stopped competing in Canton in 2000. But they still travel the country to inflate and fly the Lady Jester along with other famous shape balloons. "Everyone we meet really expects to have fun, and most do," said Carson. "The beads, the colors, the excitement of ballooning, they all bring a certain reality to the festive occasion of Mardi Gras."

Carson and Martha also have a full time job as owners of Kustom Kards, USA, begun in 1992. "Martha found seventeen people that wanted balloon cards, so our printer would print a card of their balloon. Before long, we were supplying balloon cards to balloonists all over the U.S. and the world."

The Lanes have now expanded their card business to race cars, clowns, policemen, firemen, book authors ("We need to talk, JC.") and "you name it." Check out their web site at WWW.KUSTOMKARDS.COM.

While I was compiling notes for this essay, I realized I'd found my elusive cover photo for this second volume of New Orleans inspired tales. "The Lady Jester would be honored to grace the cover of your book," writes Carson.

And Brenda and I are proud to have been a part of the Mardi Gras Magic/Lady Jester experience.

Throw me somethin', Mister Balloonist!

# Kindred Spirits

I'VE MET SOME wonderful people on my book signing tours for the first volume of *Big Easy Dreamin'*. People who "got" what I was trying to say, who felt the same way I did. One particular "critic" who hadn't bothered to read the book wrote, "Some folks might not want to hear about an average guy's trips to New Orleans," to which an interviewer at Mississippi Educational Television queried, "Who?!" Thanks, Jack Sweitzer. And me, average? Puh-leeze!

Independent bookstores like Lemuria in Jackson, Mississippi, have been my best upholders. It's always a pleasure to sign at a store with a built-in clientele. Or what a rush to receive a phone call from an acquaintance who'd just finished *Big Easy Dreamin'* and wanted to tell me how it had put laughter and smiles in their day.

My biggest supporter comes all the way from White Plains, New York. But that didn't stop him and his significant other from achieving the best New Orleans fix of anyone I know.

The gang at the Garden District Book Shop (GDBS) on Prytania began telling me about this guy who kept buying multiple copies of my book to bestow on his friends. He'd told them, "This is me! This is how *I* feel!" He has a house a few blocks away from the book shop, but the gent lives in New York. Curiouser and curiouser. He and his significant other come down to the Big Easy one long weekend every month. What devotion! My kinda guy.

Somehow, I had to cross paths with my unknown admirer.

Amy, at the GDBS finally managed to pass on the man's name

(John DeMarco) and his address, to which I sent a missive of thanks. John sent me an e-mail within the week. We began corresponding about our love for the Big Easy, and within a few months, John and I had set up a weekend when we'd both be in the city to actually meet!

It was my second "bar bouncing" encounter with author Tim Dorsey (SEE *Orange Crushin*'), but I had cleared Friday night. John had invited me to join him and partner Pat at one of their favorite restaurants, Joey K's, on the corner of Magazine and Seventh.

I'd been riding my bike through the Garden District that afternoon and happened upon John and Pat's Seventh Street address. Talk about impressive! The "nickel tour" was even better.

Their manse was built in 1901 and has withstood the test of time. It represents the first half of the 20th century when multi-generations shared the home as well as later years when neighborhood property values began to soar, family patterns changed, and modern lifestyles characterized the area.

Frank Levy, the manager of a life insurance company, was the original owner. The 1901 building cost was $7,200. The house was sold in 1921 for $22,500 to Laura Chaille Jamison. After his mother died in 1946, Dr. Chaille Jamison inherited her estate. Within ten years, the value was $52,000; by 1965, it was worth $65,000. Dr. and Mrs. Robert Ryan acquired the property in 1967 for $67,500. The Ryans did extensive renovations and lived there for sixteen years before selling it to Dr. and Mrs. Charles Pearce in 1984 for $625,000: a price that reflected both the interest and preservation of the Garden District. The property was sold twice again in 1988 and 1995, before Pat and John fell in love with it in 1998.

Pat had an antiques dealer friend in New Hampshire acquire all the furnishings and ship them down. Fabulous drapery entwined with brightly-colored paint schemes make this a true Garden District delight.

I took a roll of photos to show Brenda. I knew she'd want to see the Pat Ogden/John DeMarco estate in the flesh. Brenda would get her wish as a Christmas bonus!

John and Pat drove me to Joey K's for fine meals of catfish, Creole shrimp linguine and chicken fried steak. The New York attorneys also have a French Quarter condo acquired several years prior to the big house. The apartment on the corner of Conti and Burgundy Streets has its own history. Norma Wallace, the last of the big time French Quarter madams, once used this residence as one of her brothels. John and Pat have kept the noisy yet historical neighborhood residence as a holdover for their Mardi Gras influx.

"It was a convention that initially brought us to New Orleans in October, 1990," writes John. He and Pat were introduced to the Acme Oyster House, Bayona, K-Paul's and the New Orleans School of Cooking. "We stayed at the St. Anne/Marie Antoinette Hotel on Conti Street and the weather was gorgeous. I heard the second line coming from The Famous Door; I saw the sidewalk To-Go Drink windows and thought this was my kind of place."

John and Pat survived their first Mardi Gras in 1992. "We spent hours and hours just walking around the Quarter, doing tourist stuff, and of course, hours and hours going to parades. We went home with 8 ½ pounds of beads."

One trip in 1993 included five major restaurants in three days: Commander's Palace, Mr. B's Bistro, The Palace Café, Bacco, and Bayona. In 1994, John and Pat led a group from New York on a New Orleans Gourmet Eating Tour Weekend. That led to the "Dinner of

the Decade" in December, sponsored by the James Beard Foundation. John and Pat met Emeril Lagasse "and we've been friends ever since." The Dinner Of The Decade was held at Windsor Court Hotel with Emeril as the coordinating chef.

"I think 1994 was the real turning point for us," writes John. "We got to know New Orleans as more than just tourists." The couple met many locals through the Eating Tour and the Dinner Of The Decade, who have grown into great friends. They also spent their first Thanksgiving in the Big Easy dining at Dooky Chase with John's daughter and Pat's son.

By 1995, "a real watershed year for us vis-à-vis New Orleans," the New York couple began making trips down about four or five times a year. Towards the end of their JazzFest journey, Pat was checking out the real estate section in the *Times-Picayune* from their room at the Royal Sonesta. "Pat came upon an ad for a condo…only two blocks away," writes John. She made the call and ten minutes later, they were at the Cornerstone Condo to look at a unit. "Approximately five weeks later, on a sweltering June day, we had our place in New Orleans."

The couple's New Orleans connection was cemented in 1997 during Pat's daughter's wedding in Manchester, Vermont. "The event had a New Orleans theme," writes John, featuring a Dixieland Jazz band from Pat's hometown of Pittsburgh. Now here's the best part: it was catered by Commander's Palace. "Four days before the wedding, the executive chef, the general manager, 22 captains and waiters and 110 boxes of food were all flown to Albany and trucked over to Manchester for the wedding. The Commander's crew outdid themselves!"

In early 1998, John and Pat were asked, as a favor to a friend, to view a house for sale in the Quarter. The broker involved also included some other properties on the list, one of which was a Neo-Colonial Revival on Seventh Street. "For Pat, it was love at first sight," writes John. "Two months later, the day after Mardi Gras, we had ourselves a house in the Garden District!"

A portion of the movie *Interview With The Vampire* was shot inside the Seventh Street home. The USA Network series *The Big Easy* and Lifetime's *Any Day Now* were also filmed there.

"The house may or may not have a ghost," swears John. Early on, the couple was awakened by slamming doors, always between 3:00 and 3:15 AM John also heard a woman calling out for her mother while he was in the shower; it wasn't Pat, since there was no one else in the house. Shortly thereafter, Pat went around the house explaining

that everything was going to be alright and the "ghost" need not be concerned. The door slamming and talking ceased.

John and Pat have had many excellent adventures in their Garden District abode. Most notable was during a black tie dinner for ten, prepared by the late Jamie Shannon, executive chef of Commander's Palace. Due to Jamie's smaller cooking confines, the smoke alarm went off. Even though John informed ADT Alarm Company the situation was under control, contracts stipulated ADT send the fire department. "So with ten people in tuxes and gowns in the dining room, and Jamie in the kitchen in a cloud of smoke, the firefighters entered the house in full regalia of helmets with face shields and Scott Air Packs on their backs, axes in their hands. No one batted an eye; the party went on and a great time was had by all."

The ultimate honor was bestowed on the semi-transplanted New Yorkers in September, 2002. New Orleans' famed Preservation Resource Center contacted them about opening up their place as part of the PRC's annual holiday walking tour!

I received an e-mail in mid-November from John as he frantically recalled the early Christmas decorations going up during their monthly "long weekend" visit to the Big Easy. Their next trip via the Big Apple was "PRC Walking Tour" weekend.

It was a Creole Christmas treat as Brenda, Sean and I trekked the Garden District homes December 14th. John and Pat's mansion was even more resplendent with holiday gaiety abounding. Their pride swelled throughout all the rooms. Sean got his first taste of The Columns, where we stayed the night. The kid especially enjoyed peeking over the wide second floor balcony at the streetcars passing to and fro. And of course, we partook in the Celebration in the Oaks in City Park. The lights, the rides, the season: there's nothing more joyous for a youngster (any age) during Christmas in New Orleans. (SEE *Kidstuff*.) Except maybe a tour of John and Pat's Seventh Street home.

So you never know just who you might meet in the middle of a love affair with New Orleans. I'm fortunate to be acquainted with John DeMarco and Pat Ogden, Southern-fried Yankees who are livin' la vida loca every month way down yonder in N'awlins.

And John, I still have a few copies of *Big Easy Dreamin'* left if any of your friends and co-workers need Sin City convincing . . .

# Suzie Q

BEHIND THE QUIET façade of the ageless blonde poised at the counter of the Anne Rice Collection lies a wondrous mound of gothic memories many Rice devotees would stake this woman in broad daylight for. Sue Quiroz (Suzie Q to friends) has had amazing opportunities befall her in the realm of fandom: first, as one of the founding mothers of Anne Rice's Vampire Lestat Fan Club; then, as Anne's first secretary.

The journey began back in 1988. A trio of friends and eternal fans of Rice's vampires, erotica, and gothic galavants, Sue Quiroz stood in line for over an hour with Teresa Simmons and Susie Miller at the bookstore in One Shell Square awaiting the anointed *Queen Of The Damned*. A few years earlier, Sue's sister Melanie Scott had introduced her to *Interview With The Vampire*. Melanie was out of town for this signing, but would play an integral part in the girls' future.

"While Anne was signing our books, we told her we were thinking about starting a fan club for her," Sue recalls. "She smiled and said, 'Lestat would love that.'" The ladies borrowed paper and a pencil from the store and began taking names and addresses of fans in line to mail them newsletters of Anne's upcoming appearances in person, print or TV.

Then the big payoff: "We were invited to her house and given names and phone numbers of her agent and publisher!" A secretary at a local law firm, Sue became the main lady phoning Anne for

newsletter info. "When I lost my job, I called her to see if she needed a secretary." Anne was on tour at the time but Sue remained persistent. "The rest is history."

Susie, Teresa, Melanie and Sue had entered a world both exciting and bizarre. Rice's fan base was beginning to broaden, thanks in part to the fan club. Melanie became the first club president. Teresa took over when Mel's school work began to monopolize most of her time. Teresa served for a couple years, and then it was Sue's turn. "But Anne asked me not to do it, since I worked her for," Sue explained. "So Susie Miller took up the lead." A few years later, Ritchie Champagne would take the helm as head vampfan.

Annual Coven Parties were held each Halloween weekend to celebrate Rice and her latest gothic bestseller. Melanie often embellished her designs on party T-shirts. These Gatherings began small and intimate, but in the ensuing years, would mushroom into revelers of over 2,500.

Anne would forge multi-million dollar deals with Knopf Publishing, affording her family the luxury of a Garden District mansion. Susie came aboard as a staff member at the lavish purple estate on the corner of First and Chestnut Streets.

Additional properties were acquired: the square block occupied by St. Elizabeth's Orphanage on Napoleon Avenue, the guest house on the corner of Third and St. Charles, a refurbished home on Amelia and St. Charles, and The Happy Hour Theatre on Magazine Street. Anne hoped to turn the old theatre into The Club Lestat. The Happy Hour was later re-sold. "There was simply too much work to do on it," remembers Sue.

The first time I saw Sue and the other founding mothers was in a Rice fanzine from Innovation Comics in 1991. They graced the final pages, vamping it up in the French Quarter, proudly exposing their black leather and lace and custom fangs. Anne Rice's Vampire Lestat Fan Club info and dues were also included. I entered the ranks and have been taking party pictures ever since. Over the years, I've seen (and heard about) the other three ladies sporadically, but I've never lost contact with Suzie Q.

She was, after all, the closest spokesperson to one of my favorite authors. But I also have a lot of admiration for Sue, not just as a person, but as a bastion who's survived the maelstrom of the world of Anne Rice, holding her head high despite the unpredictable daily chaos that comes with the territory.

Depending on the year (or the mood), Sue's shoulder-length blonde (or red) tresses crowned her black lace dress as she sat dutifully next to Anne at signings around the country. Suzie Q's seen the inside of Rice's black limo more times than all its chauffeurs combined. She's strutted with an umbrella down Washington Street behind a mule-drawn hearse at both of Anne's jazz funeral/book signings. She's been mother superior to hundreds of dolls in Anne's extravagant collection. She's comforted Rice as a friend when the author's father passed away.

In the nearly ten years she served as confidant, companion, errand runner, gal Friday, right-hand lady, patron, sympathizer, and simply Suzie Q, Rice's first secretary has had a remarkable ride.

I once remarked to Sue that she could churn out a great little "tell-all" book about her time at Rice's side. But she never will; Sue has too much class. Besides, would you want The Vampire Lestat breathing (and biting) down *your* neck? Still, Sue does have some great Vampire Chronicles she was willing to share.

Like her first unplanned solo flight to Washington, D.C., during Rice's 1995 *Memnoch, The Devil* tour. Sue was busy working on projects at First Street when she got the call from Anne. "Go home now and pack was my assignment for the day," remembers Quiroz. "The limo would pick me up at home and bring me to the airport. I didn't have time to be scared."

Sue had only been on a plane a couple times, and never alone. "When I arrived, I had my first mission: buy several wigs then call Anne with what I had found." A combination of Yellow Pages, limo driver and wig store produced the scavenger hunt items for Quiroz's quirky author. Sue quickly learned how to pack better and take less.

And after getting locked out of her hotel room, Sue's boss shared the timeless "open dead-bolt, key in the PJ's" trick.

Anne Rice has made numerous TV appearances; her favorite venue was *The Rosie O'Donnell Show*. On one occasion, Sue recalls, "they let me go into the green room and wait. When Anne was getting ready to go on, I was taken out into the hall." Sue was backing up to avoid a passing group and got her foot caught in a cable. Her savior was the actor Kurt Russell. Sue fell into Russell's arms. "I hope I said thanks because I was so embarrassed, my face was red."

When Rice found out, she hit Quiroz on the arm and remarked, "Those arms, you were in those arms!" The following year, *Rosie* personnel didn't let Sue into the green room. "Lesson learned: don't fall into the arms of any actor Anne loves."

Suzie Q made it on national television when Anne appeared as herself on *Ellen*. "Anne asked if I could be in line for the booksigning scene at Ellen Degeneres' TV bookstore," said Sue. "I was thrilled and gladly held my book as a true fan would."

In the fall of 1997, Anne decided to go on a bus tour. Her latest offering, *Servant Of The Bones*, took Rice, Sue and assorted staffers across the U.S., much like a travelling band. "When we left New York at the beginning of the tour, all the publicity staff from Knopf came on the bus for a send-off."

It was a lot easier for Anne and Sue to be bussed than to travel by plane every two or three days. "Anne could get up, go to the back of the bus, get under the covers and sleep for most of the trip," Sue said. "We (the staffers) usually didn't sleep, but sat on big couches in front by the driver." They listened to stories the driver told them, watched movies on TV, or simply viewed America. "I have a new appreciation for people who tour."

Sue believes the *Servant Of The Bones* entourage traveled to at least thirty cities; Memphis' Graceland was a particularly fun stop. A hurricane nearing Miami cut the tour short; the driver brought an exhausted Rice and krewe back to New Orleans, barely missing a crepe myrtle as he nimbly pulled the huge bus into the courtyard at St. Elizabeth's.

In 1999, after ten years of adventures, Sue's duties with the Rice family were altered. She was sequestered at St. Elizabeth's where Sue became curator of Rice's doll museum. Sue also began working several days a week at the Anne Rice Collection, not far from the

First Street residence. As I stood beside her atop the second floor balcony of St. Elizabeth's viewing the approach of Anne's carriage for a 2000 booksigning of *Merrick*, it was obvious Suzie Q missed her position next to the vampire queen. Sue's replacement, albeit short lived, was Anne's goddaughter Brandy.

Rice decided to liquidate her vast doll collection in 2002 as well as the property encasing St. Elizabeth's. Until it went out of business April 19 of 2003, Sue could be seen behind the Anne Rice Collection's counter five days a week. She still has an internet business, SAGEBRUSHONLINE.COM, that offers custom jewelry and spiritual healing.

At Halloween time in 2002, Suzie Q began a revival of the almost-defunct Anne Rice's Vampire Lestat Fan Club with a Gathering at the Howlin' Wolf. Sue was nervous as a newly resurrected vampire, poised mere inches from the pouring rain, wondering if she'd at least break even on her endeavor. The crowd of 250 was reminiscent of the earlier days: orderly, cool, and spirited gothic fun. Sue's son, daughter and their significant others smiled proudly at mom's handiwork. It was a new beginning.

Whatever the future has in store for Sue Quiroz, Anne Rice will be probably be a part of it. Rice recently asked Sue to be her "special personal assistant" after Anne's gastrointestinal surgery in the spring of 2003. "It all happened pretty quick," Sue said. "I'm helping Anne with her diet management and insulin. And I'll be typing up her bibliography when she starts writing. Whatever she needs."

And when Anne Rice feels the time is right to do another book tour, I look forward to seeing the quiet blonde at her side, smiling sweetly at the panorama of fans, cameras and media heaping praise on Suzie Q's boss: the Queen Of The Damned.

# *Orange Crushin'*

TIM DORSEY ain't right. It's not his fault. He's seen things; freaky things. As a longtime nightly news coordinator for the *Tampa Tribune*, Dorsey's had his head crammed with every kind of flotsam the Florida tides might haul in.

At some point, you just can't contain it. There's tales to be told. Weird tales. Tales that might grind the rest of the country to a halt. But in the Sunshine State, it's just plain life.

Elmore Leonard, Carl Hiassen and Laurence Shames have made a killing weaving barbed beachside bestsellers based on Florida's sun-friend antics. Tim Dorsey goes five steps further. He's reinvented his own sandblaster, seat belt not included. Dorsey's hits *Florida Roadkill* and *Hammerhead Ranch Motel* broke the mold with a Hunter Thompson meets Quentin Tarantino deathride across the citrus state. His spree-killing folklorist Serge A. Storms isn't your typical tour guide. But then, neither is Tim.

I met Dorsey at a Jackson, Mississippi book signing and in turn, spread the literary word to my friends at the Garden District Book Shop (GDBS). Ted (of the GDBS) already knew Tim when he lived in Florida. Deb and Amy (other GDBS employees) met Dorsey at the Mid-South Booksellers Conference in New Orleans within months of when I did.

Now a year had passed and the Florida author was about to descend on the Big Easy once again. His new book was entitled *Orange Crush*.

"The style becomes tighter and more confident," I wrote in my Jackson *Clarion-Ledger* review, "but the radioactivity is still hovering. Dorsey fills *Orange Crush* with enough mixed nuts and dangling chads to keep you hooting for weeks."

Witnessing Tim's manic unpredictableness is almost as entertaining as reading his books. In a well-guarded corner of the French Quarter, plans were being cultivated to make his visit a most memorable one.

Local artist and scarf designer Janice Cartier used her connections at the Ritz Carlton on the corner of Iberville and Dauphine to secure a surprise party with matching drink. A devoted Dorsey junkie, Janice coaxed one of the bartenders, Kevin, to concoct an Orange Crush cocktail in Tim's (and the book's) honor.

Dorsey was driving in from the Mississippi gulf coast Friday evening prior to his Saturday signing. Needing any excuse for a New Orleans rendezvous, I nabbed an invite to Tim's Orange Crush Surprise.

After a pleasant afternoon of Quarter browsing, I rode over to the Ritz with Deb and her husband Keith. We hooked up with Amy and Ted and toured the sumptuous surroundings with Janice in the lead. Ted's roommate Cindy, a head-turning blond, met us outside the elevator. Cindy has one of the most unusual jobs in New Orleans: she greets and tours arriving conventioneers in a variety of get-ups, from Marilyn Monroe to a vampire princess. But that's another story…

It was almost 8:00 PM, time to mosey upstairs to the French Quarter Bar (FQB).

Talk about class, that's the FQB. Brass and mahogany, lots of ambiance. Come as you are. Tim wandered in a few minutes after 8:00 dressed in khaki shorts and a blue tropical shirt (his standard Florida attire). Our ever-growing entourage (now including Britton Trice, the owner of the GDBS, and his wife Ann) moved into a larger room adjacent to the bar's stage. Friday night's entertainment, Jeremy Davenport (one of the city's premier trumpeters with a Harry Connick attitude), began to serenade the bar patrons as Tim's big surprise was carried into the room.

Kevin, Janice's bartender pal, was all smiles with his silver tray of Orange Crushes. He was greeted with a rousing ovation. The thin, slightly balding young man mixed orange juice, triple sec, vodka and lime to produce a pleasingly light elixir. Dorsey grinned as he a proposed a toast to his New Orleans affiliates.

After numerous rounds, photos, and Jeremy Davenport encores, we pitched in to settle the tab and made plans for the next leg of the evening. Tim wanted to go bar hopping around the Quarter. I'd heard rumors about this guy's "hopping"...they're all true.

"One bar, one drink" was the author's rule. Dorsey escorted us from the Ritz to the Napoleon House at 500 Chartres, a bar revered by locals and tourists alike. The house was supposedly built as a refuge for the exiled Emperor Napoleon, but he never quite made it. One could wile away the hours here, intermingled with ghosts of barflies past. Yet with his last swig of Abita Amber, Tim turned to the group. "Ready?" he asked.

We whooshed into the throng of slow-moving tourists. Dorsey knew right where he wanted to drink next: Marie Laveau's Voodoo Bar. Situated across from the Jax Brewery at 501 Decatur, the Voodoo Bar takes up a small portion of The Historic French Market Inn. Tiny, private, and never a crowd, Marie Laveau's sports fetish dolls and voodoo T-shirts. It's a favorite of touring writers.

Tim ordered bourbon shooters for our dwindling entourage. I winced between swallows of Old Kentucky Tavern and my Dixie longneck. Before the gris-gris began to settle, we were off and trotting. Time to pay a call on Jean Lafitte.

Lafitte's Blacksmith Shop Bar and Patio is one of the most well known taverns in the Quarter. "The Lafitte brothers—pirates and smugglers—once operated here (1780-1825)," boasts their black and silver matchbook. "It was in this famous 941 Bourbon address that the meeting of Dominique You and Lafitte took place. Governor

Claiborne offered a reward for the Lafitte; Lafitte offered a reward for the governor. Hospitality is 'on the loose.'"

By now, I was starting to feel the effects of my beer and whiskey tango. So, of course, I ordered a strawberry daiquiri in a Lafitte's souvenir cup. The gang at the piano bar was sloppily serenading a birthday or two, so I drifted over. After fifteen minutes of losing myself in history and frozen rum, I realized I might have lost my tour as well. A smattering of familiar faces were confined in the shadows. I wobbled their way.

"The Hummingbird!" Tim bellowed over the noise.

Five tightly wound patrons packed a cab that cruised up St. Charles Avenue. Tim was ready for a late night breakfast of the grease-stricken variety. The Hummingbird Café at 804 St. Charles Avenue is "a greasy spoon in every sense of the word, from the atmosphere to the food," according to *Offbeat* Magazine. "Oily burgers and eggs are produced at the grill, in addition to other culinary wonders…In the olden days, the adjoining, ultra-cheap hotel was used by prostitutes." The Hummingbird closed its doors in the fall of 2002.

The wee hours were approaching; Tim's signing was at 1:00 PM. We shuffled back to the Ritz where our chariots awaited, and slowly rolled home for the night.

A thunderstorm dampened Dorsey's appearance several hours later. But he adorned his Orange Crush buds with book jacket T-shirts and a fond visit at the store. Near the end of Tim's signing, I got whimsical and decided to take a rainy streetcar ride up and down St. Charles; the trolley stop was only a couple blocks away. Drizzle whipped across my forearm through the open window; the cool air, a soothing retreat from my meandering hangover. Ah, this is the real New Orleans, I thought to myself.

When I returned, Tim had already left. He'd headed off to Florida for his next signing. But I knew I'd see him the following year. And even as I swore that rainy afternoon I'd never "bar bounce" with Tim Dorsey again, a little voice in the pit of my skull insisted that Napoleon Bonaparte, Marie Laveau, the Lafitte brothers and a little Hummingbird would roll out their respective red carpets for me and my wallet on the 2002 *Triggerfish Twist* Tour.

But that's another story…

*Cindy and her coconuts*

# Cin's City

I'VE NEVER INTERVIEWED someone while they were taking a bath, but I'll do almost anything for an interesting story. Cindy's got three (or four) of the most unusual jobs in the Big Easy. She's in between gigs right now and can't talk long. It's near three o'clock on a humid pre-Halloween weekend and Cindy has to be at the airport by four. She's up to her neck in suds and the only thing keeping me from drooling is…I'm on the other end of the phone several blocks away.

We had an interview and photo session set up for three, but I thought I'd call ahead first. Cindy's roommate Ted works at the Garden District Book Shop. He passes the phone my way. Cindy's all apologetic and hopes we can reschedule. With her hectic pace, doing a face-to-face won't be happening this visit.

"I could swing by real quick and snap some shots of you in costume or standing by your famous coconuts," (or in the bathtub, I think to myself). "It won't take long."

But that didn't work. "It's just weird timing all around," she moans. Cindy says she'll call me Sunday afternoon when I get back home. The morning job will be finished and the evening's activities won't commence until 5:00. She never called. I wasn't surprised.

I met Cindy during author Tim Dorsey's *Orange Crush* tour in 2001 (SEE *Orange Crushin'*). She was describing her job as a Reveleer for Carl Mack Presents. Cindy greets visiting conventioneers at the airport or at their hotels posing as famous personalities or New

Orleans-themed characters. Keep in mind Cindy's just turned fifty, has two grandkids, waist-length blonde hair, looks like a 28 year old, and runs on pure adrenaline.

Six months later, it's Mardi Gras 2002. We're hanging out at the house Cindy and Ted share on the river side of Eighth Street. Cindy sits amid a mound of beads cuddling her new grandbaby; her daughter smiles proudly from a nearby chair. Cindy's artful tilework graces the fireplace; that's another sideline. On a bureau across the room rests at least eight Zulu coconuts. "She gets one every year," says Ted, who wishes he could nab at least one. But then, Ted doesn't look like Cindy.

Cindy Kelly was born in Bentonville, Arkansas, home of Wal-Mart. She lived in Gulf Breeze, Florida for nearly ten years. That's when Cindy met Ted O'Brien; he was the manager of a Books-A-Million.

Cindy migrated northwest to the Crescent City in '99. Ted followed suit five months later after his divorce. He'd visited JazzFest and became smitten with the city and its music. When Ted's roomie moved back to Florida, he and Cindy decided to co-habit the house on Eighth Street to save on expenses. They share a great friendship and lots of love for the Big Easy.

Cindy's artistic touches are evident throughout the shotgun house she and Ted rent a block or two from Magazine Street. A Mardi Gras tree stands near the front window. Kitchen cabinets are painted with scenes from favorite places like Paris and Key West. Tiny white lights twinkle from the ceiling in the petite bathroom down the hall. Framed paintings and prints garnish the walls. I wish I had Cindy's imagination and Ted's surroundings.

"I'm just a jack of all trades," Cindy laughed when I commented on her multiple occupations. Besides being a Reveleer, she also designs headpieces for Carl Mack Presents. Then there's the new gig: Cindy works a burlesque show on Bourbon Street. Not as a dancer, mind you, but back stage. But even at fifty, she could pull it off, no pun intended. Cindy's in charge of costumes, an extension of her design artistry.

The Reveleer job is the one that pays the rent. Cindy and other revel-minded personnel get dolled up in whatever the client calls for: a Mardi Gras jester theme, an Anne Rice vampiress, Marilyn Monroe or Bette Davis (that's under Celebrity Look-a-likes). She's even created an enormous cabbage head that sits atop buffet tables, a Talking Buffet Head, as it were. Cindy's real head is in the middle. "Clients often try to dissect my cabbage," Cindy laments.

Carl Mack Presents is one of New Orleans' premiere entertainment groups. Their web site (www.carlmack.com) features dozens of colorful photos of entertainers like balloon sculptors, belly dancers, big heads, can-can dancers, caricaturists, cigarette girls, celebrity look-alikes, clowns, contortionists, female impersonators, jesters, jugglers, human statues, little people, magicians, mimes, psychics, puppeteers, musical acts, Santa's, showgirls, and of course, the Reveleers.

"Liven up your next event with our energetic and colorful Mardi Gras Reveleers," touts the site. "Meet and greet, pose for photo ops, or parade your guests to any venue, complete with brass band." Hey, if it ain't Carnival time, they'll create one for you!

I think Cindy (and Ted) have found a niche in New Orleans. Besides the Bohemian and devil-may-care attitude the city exudes, it's the music that keeps these fans rooted to the Crescent City. Ted has an almost encyclopedic knowledge of local bands and catches them as often as possible on his book-shop salary.

Cindy sees the local legends up close and personal, even when she's not trying to. "I was running errands the other day and stopped by a friend's art gallery," she recalls. "All of a sudden (pianist) John Cleary walks in, sits down at the piano and gives us a private concert." Cindy reminisces about her quirky career. "I've had thousands of photos taken of me from all over the world, in various costumes and poses," she says. "I've never seen any of them." (She'll see the ones I eventually took for this book.)

Cindy promises to do a photo shoot with me next time I come down. If I can catch up with her. Maybe I'll get lucky and snap her in the bathtub…in full Reveleer garb…with all her coconuts. Well, two out of three ain't bad.

# Stan

*September 1, 2002*

A friend I haven't heard from in a while called me around nine tonight. We're both Anne Rice and vampire fans. Janis was excited about the Halloween party the remnants of Anne's fan club were putting together October 25th at the Howlin' Wolf on North Peters. She went on and on about this vampire author and that vampire character 'til I was beginning to run out of patience (as well as blood). After about a half hour, Janis unveiled the true purpose of her call…and the reason she'd been hesitating for so long.

Janis had bad news. Real bad news. Stan Rice has two brain tumors, she told me. Both inoperable. One is at the base of his spinal cord. He was going into aggressive chemo- and radiation therapy. Stan was very optimistic and was ready to fight the good fight.

That part of the conversation lasted all of three minutes. And then we parted, promising to look one another up at the party; to keep in touch about Anne's husband.

I hung up and walked around the house stunned. It was nearly ten o'clock and I knew I'd have a hard time sleeping. It just wouldn't seem real not having Stan around. The quiet, gentle man who always sat by his wife at booksignings or stood in the shadows at parties. Handsome, roguish, unassuming. An almost devil-may-care confidence. After all, this was the flesh and blood gent that Anne had patterned for her infamous Vampire Lestat.

Lestat was quite the scoundrel in *Interview With The Vampire*. Tom Cruise never did him justice in the movie. But observing Stan from a distance: dashing in his tux in a Mardi Gras crowd; a prideful smirk standing with son Chris at one of dad's art showings; surrounded by nieces and nephews in the living room of his guest house; collecting a moment of solitude in the darkness during one of Anne's fan club soirees; or total bliss seated next to his wife of over forty years at a gala wedding reception: now *that* was the Vampire Lestat. *That* was Stan Rice.

Stan and Anne were married October 14, 1961, a month before he would turn nineteen and days after Anne reached twenty. Even at such early ages, the couple was smitten with one another's unconventional styles: he, the rakish poet with commanding voice and attitude; she, the writer with a dark past.

Stan was twenty-two when one of his poems was chosen for the 25$^{th}$ anniversary commemoration of the founding of the United Nations in San Francisco. "He was soon in demand for readings and began publishing in local literary magazines," writes Katherine Ramsland in *Prism Of The Night*, her unparalleled biography of Anne. "His wild, youthful look, combined with a vigorous content of his poetry, caught people off guard."

In 1970, Stan won the Joseph Henry Jackson award for poetry. He spent his $1,500 prize on a red MG sports car. Two years later, Stan received a $5,000 grant from the National Endowment For The Arts.

By the age of twenty-seven, Stan was already a tenured professor at San Francisco State (SFSU). His first poetry collection, *Some Lamb*, was published in 1975 when he was 33. Stan used his tragic and unusual metaphors in *Some Lamb* to ease his grief after daughter Michele died of leukemia at the age of six. The following year, *White Boy* was published. This collection won $5,000 as the Edgar Allan Poe Award for poets under 45.

During that same period of grief, Anne channeled her pain in the form of a novel. When Stan finished reading the manuscript to *Interview With The Vampire*, he remarked, "Our lives are changed."

Stan spent twenty-two years at SFSU, retiring at the age of forty-six as the chairperson of the Creative Writing Department. Anne was ready to head back to New Orleans, the city of her childhood. With her substantial contracts from Knopf publishers, Stan was able to begin exploring his new talents as an artist.

Stan surprised the art world in the early Nineties with a gallery of weird and wonderful renderings that belied his razor sharp wit and ability to parody almost any theme. My all-time favorite is "Nine Attempts of Hitler As A Baby": three rows across and three down of eight rats...and an infant in the last panel.

From his colorful floral landscapes to Roy Rogers riding into the sunset to a B-movie invasion of space aliens, Stan's paintings make you laugh, make you think and make you realize just how damn good he was.

The Stan Rice Gallery opened at St. Elizabeth's in 1999. Soon after, STANRICE.COM hit the internet, allowing fans up-close glimpses at Stan's masterpieces.

When Anne got the notion to bestow her vampire protagonist on a collection of designer wines, Couvee Lestat, Stan's art graced the labels.

A collection of Stan's artwork was released in 1998 through Knopf, Anne's publisher of over twenty-five years. He even managed to coerce the book people into keeping the price an affordable $30, so everyone could purchase one.

Stan continued to work on his poetry, publishing seven books in all, including *Body Of Work* ('83); *Singing Yet* ('92); *Fear Itself* ('95); *Radiance of Pigs* ('99); and *Red to the Rind* ('02). *False Prophet* was released in 2003.

I always loved being in the same room with his work, whether it was the Rice's guest house on St. Charles and Third, the famous First Street mansion or St. Elizabeth's Orphanage on Napoleon. Stan's paintings and poetry exude so much life and energy, they will always be a living part of his spirit.

Many of these thoughts swam through my head as I lay in bed that night. Maybe he'd pull through, I prayed. Maybe he's got the guts to beat death.

Brenda, Sean and I were in New Orleans the following weekend for a booksellers convention. Reactions from our friends were varied, from the dreamers who felt Stan would pull through to the realists who knew it would just be a matter of time. Anne's recorded telephone message to her fans called Stan's Gliobastoma stage 4 tumor, "the dark shadow that has entered our lives."

I returned the weekend before Halloween, this time solo. Brenda and Sean were at a cub scout campout that unfortunately got rained

on. The first thing I did was ask about Stan.

His doctor had given him about two weeks to live.

I was shocked and saddened. Again. My threadbare hopes were dashed.

It was a pleasant weekend, but most thoughts and conversations were focused on Stan. Signed prints of his artwork were still available at the Anne Rice Collection on Prytania. Sue Quiroz, Anne's personal assistant for many years, auctioned off a print at the fan-club party. The vamps and witches who swayed to the sounds of the Necro-tonz and Fingercuff didn't seem to fathom the implications of Stan's eminent demise.

But I did.

Anne appeared on the Today Show a day before All Hallows Eve, touting her new offering, *Blackwood Farm*. The interview had been taped at First Street a few days earlier; there was no way Anne would leave Stan in his final days. The new soon-to-be bestseller featured the Vampire Lestat and a new creature of the night, Quinn Blackwood, whom Anne had based on son Chris. Even with a tragedy of darkest proportions looming on their doorstep, Anne had managed to unite the family together in her grand gothic style.

"We will always be together," Anne told the interviewer when questioned about Stan. "We are beyond death."

*December 4, 2002*

Another call from Janis. They're taking Stan to the hospital today; it's down to the wire now. Janis said the Rice family is making funeral arrangements. Damn. He won't even get to enjoy the holidays.

So this is it. Right when we're all in the middle of the insanity that is Christmas. No time to think, not much time to pray. Not much time to grieve, either. I'm sure I'll miss the funeral, too, what with my frantic schedule. But I'll pass a little prayer Stan's way.

I already miss him. I'll always hold Stan close to my heart, always remember his smile and warmth. Never forget his art and poetry. And the fact that he always treated the world with kindness and respect.

That's Stan Rice. Husband to Anne. Father to Chris and Michele. Role model for The Vampire Lestat. Artist. Poet. Friend. Regular Guy.

You left this world way too soon. But I'm sure there's a canvas in one corner and a keyboard in another for you to continue your heavenly creations.

Stan Rice passed away on December 9.

§2

# *Customs*

PHOTOS BY AMY LOEWY

# Strut Your Mutt

NEW ORLEANS has gone to the dogs…for at least one Sunday two weeks prior to Mardi Gras anyway. Hundreds, if not thousands of costumed canines and their regal owners converge on Armstrong Park early in the morning on the Sabbath to commence the "Pawty" preceding the royal march through the Vieux Carre at 2:00 PM.

The King and Queen have been chosen by secret ballot a few weeks earlier; they've been through a whirlwind of activities befitting their human counterparts: costume fittings, grooming, parties, media interviews and photo shoots. They even have their own web page.

Now these poised and pampered pooches pose on velvet cushions, clad in ribbons and robes amid the pageantry that is the Krewe of Barkus.

Daschunds in dresses, beagles in beachwear, Chihuahuas in chemise, labs in leather, pitt bulls in pastel (well, maybe not). You get the idea. Forget the old-line parading groups and superkrewes; push aside thoughts of Zulus, Indians, walking clubs and virtually anything on two legs. This is a dog day afternoon, in the strictest sense of the word. Long live Barkus!

Celebrating their tenth anniversary in 2002, The Mystic Krewe of Barkus commemorated America's renewed patriotism with the theme: Freedom's Best Friend, Saluting Canine Heroes. Red, white and blue converged with purple, gold and green to give Carnival a flag-waving flavor. KING JAKE RUSSELL and QUEEN PUFFER ruffed their approval over their ardent admirers.

Barkus (the mutt connotation of the krewe of Bacchus) winds through fifteen blocks of the French Quarter. Pups and their owners parade behind the King and Queen's float, fittingly pulled by humans. Thousands turn out to walk and watch.

And to think, it all started as a joke. In November of 1992, patrons of the Good Friends Bar were gathered for a meeting of the Margaret Orr Fan Club. Orr is one of WDSU's weather anchors. Dog owner Thomas Wood carted his canine, Jo Jo McWood, to the assemblage. After patrons complained about Jo Jo's neurotic ways, Thomas decided, fine, I'll just make Jo Jo queen of her own parade and captain-for-life.

A few days later, the gesture didn't sound so silly. Wood and friends decided to create a real Mardi Gras krewe of parading dogs. Get a permit and everything. They dubbed it the Krewe of Barkus.

The first meeting was held on January 25, 1993, at Good Friends Bar, naturally. The inebriated founders officially elected Jo Jo McWood QUEEN BARKUS I. Scott Freeman's dog Jager was voted KING BARKUS I. The inaugural theme was Welcome To The Flea Market. The first Barkus parade was a small, albeit, howling success.

Jurassic Bark was chosen as 1994's Barkus theme. The parade route was now eight blocks long. His Majesty Bark-tina became KING BARKUS II. Jo Jo remained queen.

The comrades at Good Friends Bar knew they had something important on their paws. Interest was flowing like Kibbles and Bits. The Louisiana SPCA got involved as well as other organizations for the rehabilitation and survival of strays and throwaways. Barkus was gaining respectability, and dogs were being saved.

By 1995, thousands of pooches portraying Hollywood's heyday strutted to Lifestyles of the Bitch & Famous. A seven year old English Bulldog named His Majesty Rex was crowned KING BARKUS III.

Attendance records were house-broken in 1996 for the fourth annual Tails From The Crypt. Dogs dressed in drag growled through this monstrous theme. Lola, a cage-bound throwaway at the LA/SPCA, rose from rags to QUEEN BARKUS IV.

QUEEN SYLVIA V and KING DELTA V ruled 2001: A Dog Odyssey in 1997. The dog duo was special that year; from tragedy sprang royalty. Sylvia had been thrown from a car window as a pup, then rescued by an LA/SPCA employee. Once a "psychotic, vicious beast," Delta received special canine counseling on his path to kingship. His motto: "Life is short, bite hard."

One of the wettest parades of the century, 1998's Tailtanic, requested dogs and children first. 007: From Barkus With Love spied in 1999. Joan of Bark got medieval in 2000, featuring the first-ever king/queen float—pulled by humans, of course. KING OSCAR VIII and QUEEN PASHA VIII were featured royalty. Saturday Bite Fever discoed in 2001. Pups in Elvis attire twisted to the "Jailhouse Bark" in 2003.

In over a decade on the streets, Barkus has taken a bite out of the hearts of New Orleanians. Kindness, creativity and fun has always been the focus behind the dogma of rehabilitation and contributing to the paws.

Care to be a krewe member? It's only $15. Membership is open to all dogs regardless of their past. Pre-registration for the parade is $30. The early Dogluxe package includes dues and registration. You can still register the day of the parade for $40. Additional human escort passes are $5 each.

If you'd like your pup to be considered for a place on the Royal Court as Duke or Duchess, submit a doggie bio and nomination request. Spaces are extremely limited, and there's a $250 court fee if your pet becomes a lucky dog.

Jo Jo McWood is always Captain...but you knew that.

The chartered, licensed, non-profit, all-dog krewe starts its procession from Armstrong Park, pausing at the reviewing balcony at Good Friends Bar. VIP's (including New Orleans city officials and other important humans) toast the royal court. There's even a black-tie optional party. The Barkin' Up The Ritz Ball is held at the Ritz Carlton and costs $75 per human. Sorry, no four legged friends allowed. Parade and T-shirt proceeds are donated to a worthy animal welfare group or groups.

To strut your mutt or to dig more dirt on the Mystic Krewe of Barkus, call (504) 666-2788, (504) 586-8686 or (504) 581-BARK. Or howl at their on-line history at BARKUS.ORG.

*Naughty, baudy fun with the Krewe du Vieux*

# Krewe With A Vieux

THEY COME CAVORTING up the street like the cast of a Fellini movie; wildly costumed, over the edge bawdiness. Pulling insanely decorated floats that parody the town with ribald wickedness: a hint of the past shot into the drunken new millennium. Old ladies stand aghast, their eyes bulging, mouths ajar. Parents cover their children's eyes and usher them down side streets; they weren't meant for this.

But the majority of onlookers sip their drinks and smile, their pulse quickening, cold breath emanating beneath centuries old Vieux Carre balconies.

It's the new year and the true herald to Carnival has arrived.

Unless you're a local or an unsuspecting tourist who happens to be in New Orleans a few weeks ahead of the big Mardi Gras parades, you might never get the chance to experience the manic, creative and totally unbridled debauchery of The Krewe du Vieux.

Usually within a parade, I'll focus on one or two people who have that marching attitude: the energy and wild abandon that make them stand out from the other revelers. In the case of the Krewe du Vieux, there are no standouts. They're *all* running on pure adrenaline and lots of alcohol.

From their multi-layered and laugh out loud web site (KREWEDUVIEUX.ORG) one can glean lots of information. It all started in 1978 as the Krewe of Clones, a "wild, satirical" group culled from members of the New Orleans Contemporary Arts Center (CAC). The

Krewe Of Clones paraded in the French Quarter, much like 1800's krewes: smaller, decorative and parody-driven.

In 1986, a lot of in-fighting among the krewe and CAC members, not to mention pressures from the city concerning its parade night being prior to the next day's Super Bowl, caused the Krewe of Clones to call it quits.

But it wasn't over. Two sub-krewes of the Clones (The Krewe of Underwear and the Krewe of Mama Roux) held a "Clone funeral." "An anatomically correct (and erect) clone was created and placed on a funeral cart, and a short march to a party site was planned." But wouldn't you know it, one of the biggest troublemakers at the CAC caught wind and called the New Orleans Police Department (NOPD). Eleven cop cars converged on the "unauthorized march" and forced the costumed mourners to parade on the sidewalk. The group was heard to say that no one could've cleared the streets any better for their march.

A few weeks later, during Fat Tuesday festivities, two other sub-krewes (The Seeds of Decline and the Krewe of CRUDE) decided on an informal march through the Quarter. Their fitting theme: The Stupor Bowl.

The two groups (four sub-krewes) banded together and set an official parade date three Saturdays before Mardi Gras (The Krewe of Clones' original time). They obtained a permit and renamed themselves the Krewe du Vieux Carre, later shortened to the Krewe du Vieux.

The first captain was Craig "Spoons" Johnson, a member of the Krewe of Underwear. Susan Gilbeault assisted Johnson the second year. By year three, Ray "Plaine" Kern began a ten year service as captain. The krewe grew from 150 "drunks stumbling through the French Quarter in search of a bar" to 600 "relatively" organized but still drunk participants. And an actual parade route was established.

The KduV's floats are hand made and hand-or-mule drawn, much like the golden days of Mardi Gras. A legion of brass bands play between sub-krewes and their floats. The parade begins on Decatur in the Faubourg Marigney, then proceeds through the Quarter, winding all the way up to Canal and the krewe's party spot. In 2002, the State Palace Theatre served as the host for the Krewe du Vieux Doo. A brass band jam, culminated from all the parading bands, plus

Papa Grows Funk and late night with Janet Lynn and the Red, Hot & Blues brought the revelry to a screaming head. The Vieux Doo is one of the premiere throwdowns of Mardi Gras season.

The 2002 theme was Brave New World, based on Alexander Huxley's novel. This group of bad pun freaks turned it into a free for all, aimed directly at the heart of city politics. Just a smattering of themes include Depravedheart, Keep the Jive Alive, Send in the Clones, Depraved Moo World (a krewe of cows), Krewe du Jieux attends Hogwarts Yeshiva (complete with their coveted golden bagels), Comatose Licks the Habit (nun debauchery) and Rue Bourbon has a Super Bowel Movement.

In their web newspaper, *Le Monde de Merde* (Purple prose, yellow journalism and the lust for green) the visitor can read through a dozen pages of mirth and gain info on every sub-krewe in du Vieux.

Besides the four founding groups, other revelers include the Krewe of Space Age Love, Krewe of LEWD (Lewd Ensemble of Weird Degenerates), Drips and Discharges, TOKIN (Totally Orgasmic Krewe of Intergalactic Ne'er-do-wells), KAOS (Kommittee for the Aggravation of Organized Society), the Knights of Mondu, Krewe of Rue Bourbon, CRAPS (Craps Relates Alien Phish Stories), PAN (Perpetuating Adolescent Naughtiness), Krewe du Jieux, Mystic Krewe of Spermes, Krewe of Comatose and the Mystic Krewe of Inane.

Somehow, I don't feel this will be required learning in Louisiana History classes. But for a group so well organized, yet so drunk, rising from the ashes of inebriated defeat and spreading cheer to chilly patrons on a winter's night in N'awlins, here's hoping The Krewe du Vieux's antics will propel it well into the next millennium.

# Braggin' In Brass

*(A portion of this essay appeared in* The Jackson Free Press, *Jackson, Miss., Dec. 18, 2002)*

Another of my heavenly scenarios involves wandering down Decatur Street towards the Café du Monde and happening upon the sweet refrains of a brass band. They're standing on the corner, kickin' it in high gear, each member firing out a hot solo, daring the next to improve upon the moment.

A crowd begins to gather, swaying to the sounds, clapping and singing along. Movements become more accelerated and soon the whole group is groovin' like a Tuesday night at the Maple Leaf Bar.

The band finishes their song to thunderous ovation, then spreads out in a line formation. "Y'all wanna second line?" the tuba player asks the appreciative audience. Handkerchiefs and umbrellas whip out of nowhere and we play "follow the leader" towards the Moonwalk overlooking Big Muddy.

Brass bands have been a part of New Orleans culture for well over 150 years, chronicled as early as 1850. Every small town has had its brass band, made up of firemen, police officers, high school and civic groups that gather and play to commemorate patriotic holidays. In the Big Easy, brass is a way of life.

These talented musicians are incorporated into everyday activities, especially funerals, giving the dearly departed a rousing send-off and spreading a feeling of joy throughout the mourners. I've had more than a few friends wish for an authentic New Orleans jazz funeral when they pass. Anne Rice has already had a couple brass band led funerals on her way to a booksigning from Lafayette Cemetery Nº 2 to the Garden District Book Shop. The recent jazz funeral of R&B great Ernie K-Doe incorporated most of the city's brass to give Mr. "Mother-In–Law" a heavenly hello.

New Orleans' social aid and pleasure clubs depend on the men and women of brass to lead them in their annual parades throughout their neighborhoods. Brass bands herald Mardi Gras parades, mother's day marches, Mardi Gras Indians, grand openings, festivals, and even Mal's St. Paddy's Parade in Jackson, Mississippi.

In the early days, members of a marching unit dressed alike in white shirt, black tie and black or white captain's hat with the band's name across the front. Black pants and coat completed the uniform. Groups like The Camelia, The Hurricanes, The Eureka, The Excelsior, The Onward, The Reliance, and The Young Tuxedo Brass Band are just a trickle of the entertainment served up Crescent City style in the first half of the twentieth century.

While there are still several dignified "old school" groups like The Liberty and The Treme, the brass band renaissance begun in the early 1970's is a whole 'nother matter.

T-shirts, jeans, sneakers, and a funky attitude incorporate the new look and sounds of the New Orleans brass band. Though well received

by music lovers in the Seventies, it took another twenty years for the Big Easy music scene to erupt in an epiphany of brass.

The Dirty Dozen Brass Band recently celebrated twenty-five years of burning a hole in the stereotype. Culminated in 1977, the group borrowed its name from the Dirty Dozen Kazoo Band, a group of Sixth Ward Mardi Gras revelers who played kazoos and beat drums at Carnival time and at house parties. Utilizing brass band standards, then injecting them with modern jazz, R&B and funk, The Dozen began a legacy that has influenced and spawned one of the finest collections of next generation groups since the 1920's.

Teaming up with local heroes like Dr. John and the Neville Brothers, the Dirty Dozen created new standards like The Rolling Stones' "All Over Now," "Blackbird Special," the "Flintstones" theme, and "Little Liza Jane." Many listeners were skeptical at first with the break in tradition, mixing in Michael Jackson and Herbie Hancock songs. But the more the Dozen played and toured, the more the world caught on to this electrifying new sound. With each album, the Dirty Dozen experimented with new blends of old and new, further cementing their mark on the brass band block.

Although members have changed over the years, saxophonist Roger Lewis, trumpeter Efrem Towns and sousaphonist Julius McKee still hold the threads of the early Dozen together. The Dirty Dozen has toured the world over: thirty countries and five continents, and boast nine albums. Wherever the Dozen play, audiences rarely leave the dance floor.

A year before The Dirty Dozen's 1984 debut album, "My Feet Can't Fail Me Now," a couple of high school friends were rounding up their own group, and beginning to add a whole lot of rebirth and attitude to the brass band scene.

In 1983, brothers Phillip and Keith Frazier, along with Kermit Ruffins, formed the Rebirth Brass Band, a ragtag bunch of kids with talent, funk and plenty of raucous energy. Their signature theme, "Do What You Wanna," has become a Mardi Gras staple. With Frazier's punchy sousaphone base lines and Ruffins' uncanny ability to transcend Louis Armstrong in horn, voice and charisma, The Rebirth enhanced even tighter styles originated and influenced by the Dozen.

The Rebirth suffered a minor setback when Kermit decided to venture into more traditional swing jazz. Providing barbecue from

the back of his truck, the trumpeter dubbed his new band Kermit Ruffins and the Barbecue Swingers. In short order, Ruffins has continuously won honors as the city's favorite trumpeter and swing band. He occasionally plays opposite the Rebirth in clubs like The Howlin' Wolf, Tipitina's and Vaughn's.

It didn't take long for The Rebirth (even without Ruffins) to surpass the Dirty Dozen's popularity in New Orleans. Adding new musicians, including virtuoso percussionist Ajay Mallory, the Frazier brothers and krewe rake in annual honors as the Big Easy's best brass band. Their weekly Tuesday night gig at the Maple Leaf has become legendary, often ending with the sunrise.

The Rebirth has chalked up over twenty tours of Europe, four tours of Japan and have spent six weeks in Africa. They've played virtually every music fest in the u.s. But ask any member, and they'll tell you the Maple Leaf is their gig of choice.

These days, over a dozen brass bands play clubs throughout New Orleans. The Soul Rebels, Little Rascals, Trombone Shorty, The New Birth, The Algiers, The Pin Stripe, The Potholes, The Pinettes, Bob French's Original Tuxedo Brass Band, The New Orleans Nightcrawlers, Bonearama, and others keep New Orleans hoppin'.

Besides the Maple Leaf, another great venue to catch brass bands is Donna's Bar and Grill on the corner of Rampart and St. Ann. Donna Sims and staff have a loving respect for New Orleans brass that transcends color barriers.

Whether you prefer the traditional brass at Preservation Hall and The Palm Court Jazz Café or the infectious buck jumping of the funky, hip-hop brass at Donna's, The Maple Leaf, or for tips in front of St. Louis Cathedral in Jackson Square, the Big Easy has full bragging rights.

*A social aid and pleasure club parades at Jazz Fest*

# *Social Aid*

SOME OF THE MOST anticipated events of Jazz Fest are the daily parades winding their way through the fairgrounds. You're standing in a sea of music lovers, glancing at your Fest schedule, trying to figure out how to catch three acts simultaneously while inhaling some Crawfish Monica. First you hear the brass band in the distance. Then the approaching crowd surges into a sea of happy faces and clapping hands. Band members sway and swing their trombone, bass drum, trumpet, snare and sax like the musicians of one of the great southern university marching units.

But it's the second line—the paraders that follow the band—that attracts the most attention. Colorfully clad gentlemen: their fedoras dipping with the rhythm, their neon suits garlanded with feathers and glitter, banners proudly displayed and umbrellas at the ready, or a flourish of women carrying custom made handkerchiefs with color-coordinated pantsuits laced in righteous sweat from their trek, represent two of the almost eighty social aid and pleasure clubs in the New Orleans area.

The social aid and second line clubs are like a closed society of peacocks, weaving through the streets of black communities throughout the Crescent City. Nearly every Sunday from August through June, second line parades from the small to the lavishly large, dance, strut and "buck jump" to the brassy rhythms of some of the city's funkiest ensembles.

Fest-goers and "right place at the right time" tourists are allowed a prestigious glimpse of a N'awlins tradition slow-brewed for well over 200 years. Social aid groups were formed as early as 1783 as black benevolent societies, providing a means of assistance to members, from health care to burial expenses. They were the first forms of insurance for African Americans. These "mutual aid societies" held parades as a way of advertising and to enlist others to join.

In the 1890's, "Black Carnival" was in full swing, since blacks were not allowed to parade with white society. Most second line members bought new suits, signifying the newness of life with the approach of Easter.

By the 1940's, the rise of state-run health care and black-owned insurance companies slowed the necessity of social aid clubs. But that never stopped these groups from taking to the streets. The birth of the Tambourine and Fan Clubs, AKA Social Aid and Pleasure Clubs, buoyed the proud African American heritage of brass band led marches, using a club's anniversary or the latest king and queen's coronation as excuses to parade.

Groups borrowed dress ideas from Mardi Gras Indian tribes, using feathers, tassels and stones to enhance their costume or to state their ranking. When fans weren't enough to keep away the humidity of the Big Easy, walkers brought out their umbrellas. A gaily decorated second line umbrella has become a staple for every parade, and part of the "dress code" for the social aid groups. They call 'em portable shade.

Many marches last up to four hours and stretch as far as eight miles. There are set bar stops along the way. But paraders don't drop by for a quick draft. Rest, water and bathroom breaks are the key ingredients to these tenacious second liners. It's a holdover from a time when bars would sponsor each float in the Tramps (later Zulu) parade.

The Mardi Gras parading krewe of Zulu produced one of the earliest social aid/second line clubs.

Organized in 1909, the Tramps refurbished seven years later to become Zulu walkers. With a current membership of 375 and another 175 associates, the Zulu Social Aid & Pleasure Club is the largest (and granddaddy) of the group.

Donna's Bar & Grill at 800 North Rampart is a regular watering hole for at least three second line groups. Proprietress Donna Sims' establishment is one of the mainstays for area brass bands and their constituents. This hole-in-the-wall neighborhood club bordering the Quarter is "real" New Orleans. Their barbecue is as tasty as the music.

Most social aid and second line clubs hail from the Sixth Ward, the Treme neighborhood near Armstrong Park. Others reside in Gertown, Uptown or near the Carrollton area; some groups also live on the Westbank in Algiers. Dues run from $175 to $890 annually per member, not including the multiple outfits required. Membership is fairly selective and hard to come by. Members may total only seven to almost three hundred. Each club picks out a specific Sunday to march; Easter is especially popular. You probably won't see a parade announcement in the *Times-Picayune*; if you're from the neighborhood, you know. Otherwise, you might just get lucky.

While second line and social aid clubs are virtually the same entities, walking clubs are very different. Walking clubs were formed exclusively to precede Carnival krewes. Take, for instance, Pete Fountain's Half-Fast Walkers, the first walking club you'll see on Fat Tuesday. Social aid clubs strut their stuff every Sunday, in addition to hosting raffles, dances and Queens balls.

Clubs like the Zig Zag, Lady Sequences Marching Club, Black Men Of Labor, Foe Boosters, Second Line Jammers, Divine Ladies, Valley Of Silent Men, and the Millennium Steppers carry a lot of heritage, history and pride throughout the black neighborhoods of New Orleans.

There's no better way to express yourself on a tepid Sunday afternoon than by donning your club attire and sash, grabbing an umbrella and a handkerchief, and dancing to the red-hot rhythms of a brass band. When it comes to social aid, it's worth every aching muscle, every drop of sweat, and every blister produced on weary feet.

# *Injuns*

**T**HEY ARE A CULTURE unlike any other in the world: inner city Negroes dressed in elaborate Native American costumes, loosely parading through their New Orleans neighborhoods in a cacophony of color and spectacle. Only in the Big Easy.

Over fifty gangs comprise both Uptown and Downtown tribes. Most people, especially whites, see them only during Jazz Fest. Locals eagerly anticipate Mardi Gras, St. Joseph's night, and Super Sunday parades heralded by these oddly beautiful, out of time and place craftsmen and performers. Unless you're a very lucky tourist, you've probably only seen them in a photo spread.

The Mardi Gras Indians are a dying breed, a secret society much akin to Carnival's royal krewes. They've paraded for over a hundred years but are the least recognized in Carnival lore. Once coming together in blood feuds, the tribes have put aside old scores to pay respect to one another's Big Chief and the thousands of dollars and man hours spent making their elaborate "suits."

You've heard their songs: "Iko Iko" done by The Dixie Cups and Dr. John; "Big Chief," covered by numerous groups, including Professor Longhair and The Meters; and "Hey Pockey Way" by the Neville Brothers. Most tribes have accompanying bands, The Wild Magnolias being one of the tightest. When these groups take the stage at Jazz Fest, and the chanting, the wild dancing and swirling of costumes begins, the audience becomes transfixed and transported to another time.

There have been reports of New Orleans blacks "masking Indian" as early as 1872, but the "standard" story began in the mid-1880's. After the Buffalo Bill Wild West Show stopped in the Crescent city in 1884, complete with Plains Indians, Becate Battiste and friends showed up in a Treme neighborhood bar billing themselves as The Creole Wild West. Battiste had both Native American and African bloodlines.

Many speculate the imaginary Indian tribes were created through respect from blacks toward Native Americans for their help in escaping slavery and accepting them into their society. In Trinidad, Haiti and Brazil, blacks celebrated carnival by wearing feathers, drumming and chanting.

The original Mardi Gras Indian dress was simple, copied from local tribes and Caribbean Amerindians. Gang wars were fought on "battlefronts," in other words, street corners and back alleys. Mardi Gras Day was a dangerous time, when inner city neighborhoods were filled with maskers and children…and Indians carrying sharp hatchets and knives. Police found it almost impossible to break in and break up a pitched battle.

In the 1950's, Big Chief Tootie Montana of the Yellow Pocahontas began turning tribes away from violence and more towards showmanship. Today, the Mardi Gras Indian ritual is a "living theatre of art and culture." When two tribes pass, the air is friendly yet competitive. Why ruin a $3,000 suit in a skirmish.

If you're familiar with the lyrics to "Iko Iko" and "Big Chief," you're aware of some of the ranks of the Mardi Gras Indians. The Spy Boy is the first in front, the baddest of the tribe. He usually proceeds the group by a block or two. When the Spy Boy spots another group of Indians, he sends a signal to the Flag Boy. The Flag Boy carries the tribe's colors displayed on an elaborate flag. He relays the signal down the line until it reaches the Big Chief. Signals consist of whooping, hollering, dancing and using sign language.

Mardi Gras Indian ranks also include the Spy Flag, the Gang Flag, the 1$^{st}$ and 2$^{nd}$ Flag, and the 1$^{st}$ and 2$^{nd}$ Chief. There is only one Big Chief.

It may take up to a year to complete a costume, from design and ordering material to sewing and beadwork The beads are all done by hand. A typical Big Chief suit will cost over $1,000 for the rhinestones, $320 for velvet, and hundreds more for beads and feathers. It weighs between 100 and 150 pounds. Downtown Indians use sequins and feathers while the Uptown tribes work with beads, rhinestones and feathers. The Big Chief creates a new costume each Mardi Gras, often planning a year in advance. These elaborate costumes are displayed in museums and historical societies around the world.

Due to the enormous expense of suit-making, there is always the threat of tribal extinction. Even through the generosity of neighborhood and friends, supporting a family and creating a costume keeps many a Big Chief on the warpath.

The New Orleans Mardi Gras Indian Council was formed in 1987 to help preserve the Indian culture. Presided by Larry Bannock, Big Chief of the Golden Star Hunters, the group has thrived and survived into the new millennium. Check out the Council's killer web site at MARDIGRASINDIANS.COM.

The music of the Neville Brothers was highly influenced through their Uncle Jolly, Big Chief of the Wild Tchoupitoulas (Indian translation: Mud Fish People). In their first incarnation as a band, the brothers dressed as Indians and made funky as The Wild Tchoupitoulas. Big Chief Jolly passed on a few years ago, but his spirit still resides deeply within Art, Charles, Cyril, Aaron and their offspring.

You've heard about the neighborhood Fat Tuesday parades, but Super Sunday brings all the tribes together. Held on the Sunday closest to St. Joseph's Day (March 19), the parading event is announced in local publications. As on Mardi Gras, the route is secret. The progression can be many streets long. Second liners march between ranking Indians.

Traditional meeting places are in Shakespeare Park on the corner of Washington Avenue and Lasalle Street in Uptown New Orleans and at the intersection of Orleans and North Claiborne Avenues near Armstrong Park.

When one big chief meets another, a greeting in the form of song, chant and dance is presented. A threatening challenge to "humba" (bow and respect, be humble) is demanded. The reply is a whoop and equally impressive song and dance with the retort: "Me no humba, you humba!" As the Big Chiefs pass, scars of their ancestors glaring in their eyes, they might just smile and whisper to one another, "Lookin' good…"

I've often wondered why African Americans posing as Indians would consider an Italian holiday a time to parade. As long as we can appreciate the beauty, splendor pageantry and history, the Mardi Gras Injuns can parade any day they want.

Some of the Mardi Gras Indian Tribes of Greater New Orleans: The Yellow Pocahontas; The Yellowjackets; The Creole Wild West; The Mohawk Hunters; The Golden Star Hunters; The Spirit of the Pi Yi Yi; The Wild Magnolias; The Wimbang Indians; The Little Red, White and Blue; The Golden Blades; The Wild Tchoupitoulas; The Monogram Hunters; The Guardians of the Flame; The Golden Eagles; The Ninth Ward Hunters; The White Eagles; The Black Eagles; and The White Cloud Hunters.

# Satchmo In The Summer

Now what could possibly entice you to want to head to the Big Easy in the middle of the most oppressive humidity God ever created during a month when steam rolls off the sidewalk and people seriously think about passing out rather than walk another step?

Could a birthday party for the greatest jazz legend of all time bring you down? If it were held mostly inside, would that be even better? If you were guaranteed the best music, the most scrumptious food, plus lectures that actually kept you awake, and hotel rates that couldn't be beat, might you brave the heat and humidity a Sin City summer is infamous for?

Satchmo Summerfest is beginning to change a lot of people's minds about August in New Orleans. "*What A Wonderful World* you'll discover during an edu-taining weekend" shouts the headline atop the festival's web site WWW.SATCHMOSUMMERFEST.COM. There's musical "informances" and discussions, exhibits, a jazz mass, activities for budding young jazz fans (hands-on kids' activities), a club crawl, "red beans & ricely yours" foods, and star studded performances, topped off with a second line parade that would make Louis proud. From brass bands to big bands and early jazz to Pop's All-Star sound, Satchmo Summerfest aims to please the ears, eyes and taste buds.

And get this: it's free!

Most activities congregate at the Old U.S. Mint, 400 Esplanade, on the back side of the French Market. Three stages feature Traditional Jazz, Contemporary Jazz and Brass Bands jamming from 11:00 'til 7:00. Local groups like Dr. Michael White's Liberty Jazz Band, The Dukes of Dixieland, The Donald Harrison Quartet, Jeremy Davenport, Dejan's Olympia Brass Band, The New Orleans Nightcrawlers, The Storyville Stompers, The Treme Brass Band, and Kermit Ruffins & the Barbecue Swingers join in to pay tribute to the gravelly voiced trumpeter who made Jazz a household word.

Edu-taining seminars run all day inside The Mint. From 10:00-6:00, historians both local and worldwide gather to spread the word of Satchmo in his various forms and factions. Film screenings of Armstrong's movies are a delight as well as personal recollections from record producers. Satchmo At Home explores New Orleans at the turn of the twentieth century, aided by walking tours of Louis' playing grounds and old Storyville haunts. A musical luncheon at the Palm Court Jazz Café is the perfect break.

Speaking of food, many local restaurants feature Satchmo-related delicacies all revolving around Armstrong's "red beans & ricely" signature. Some of the Red Bean Alley vendors at the Mint include Belle Forche and their *Hellzapoppin'* pulled pork po-boy with red beans and rice sauce, Greco's red bean pasta salad, Crescent City Brewhouse's red bean ice cream with a rice cookie, the Café Royal's red bean jambalaya, and Pat O'Brien's smoked chicken and red bean eggroll.

Full blown meals are touted for many eateries' Sizzlin' Satchmo Specials. Broussard's at 819 Conti features the *Gone Fishin'*: crispy fried crab over spicy red bean cake with shrimp, crabmeat and etouffee sauce. The Palace Café, 605 Canal Street, offers a *Sunset Café Stomp*: cornbread crusted gulf fish served with red beans and roasted Creole tomato succotash. Check out the *Fat Ma and Skinny Pa* at the Vernada at the Hotel Intercontinental, 444 St. Charles: crab and cornbread stuffed pork chops with a bourbon pecan glaze, cheese and herb grits, and grilled asparagus. And that's just a teaser. I almost had to stop taking notes while my mouth was watering!

Want more? There's night concerts at the City Auditorium, bringing together tons of local talent for a star-studded night of Armstrong's music.

Satchmo Summerfest (SSF) is quickly becoming a summertime favorite among locals and tourists. Begun the first weekend in August 2001 as a one-time tribute to commemorate the hundredth birthday of Armstrong (August 4), the festival's premiere success prompted producers to continue embracing Pop's legacy. In 2002, attendance doubled. Now every first weekend in August (or the weekend closest to Satchmo's birth), the music, life and history of Louis Armstrong are proudly displayed for the world to re-discover.

SSF is the only Armstrong-themed festival in the United States. Award winning posters and T-shirts are available as well as the official CD: *Louis-iana Armstrong*, featuring tributes from local musicians. Hotel rooms are priced nice for summer anyway, so here's a great reason to drop in on the Crescent City while things are hot...in more ways than one.

Satchmo Summerfest is sponsored by the Louisiana Office of Tourism, and produced by French Quarter Festivals, Inc., those fine folks who bring you the French Quarter Fest in April, and Christmas—New Orleans Style in December. Log on WWW.FRENCHQUARTERFESTIVALS.COM to check out all three.

Come next August, forget the heat and humidity; think Pops!

# Festivals Acadiens

NEW ORLEANS' CAJUN musical roots run deep...and west, of that fair city. Much of the Acadien sounds we love and love to dance to come from Lafayette and surrounding tributaries like Ville Platt, Eunice, Breaux Bridge, Mamou, and Opalouses. The spoken language is more French than English and the attitude is, "I'd rather be dancing."

One of my favorite festivals is held every third weekend in September in Gerard Park just down from the University of Southeast Louisiana. Thousands come from across the U.S. and all over the world. The food is exquisite, the attitude contagious and the bon vivant, non-stop.

My friend Peter and I discovered Festivals Acadiens a few years back. I wanted to experience firsthand what I'd read in magazines and brochures, plus take the twenty minute ride to New Iberia to visit the true-life setting of James Lee Burke's fictional Cajun cop, Dave Robicheaux.

Lafayette is about two hours from New Orleans, travelling on I-10 an hour to Baton Rouge, then another hour further west. Friends who've lived there for a time have told me how the *joie de vivre* (joy of life) is everpresent. The food is fabulous. Crawfish are plentiful; the world famous Crawfish Festival is held in Breaux Bridge, just a few miles down the road.

Restaurants, honkeytonks and dancehalls like Mulate's and Prejean's feature regional Cajun bands. They also spotlight locals who live and love to dance. These folks are serious about it, too. As I've noticed, it's an acceptable custom to dance with whomever asks you. The ladies aren't shy about it, either.

While staying in Lafayette, there are multitudes of affordable hotels and B&B's in and around town. If you're attending Festivals Acadiens, check the map and try to book a place within walking distance of Girard Park. Or park at the Cajun Dome on campus and head over.

When you're near the festival grounds, you'll begin to hear the strains of the fiddle, accordion, and *ti fers* (triangle). Your olfactory senses will perk up with the smells of etouffee, crawfish boil, shrimp jambalaya and bread pudding.

Then you'll witness the sea of dancers. Young and old, dusty and sweating, skirts swirling and bodies twirling. Non-stop two-steps and waltzes. If a bomb fell, these folks would already be in heaven.

The fest features the best Cajun bands around: Jo-el Sonnier, Balfa Toujours, Wayne Toups and Zydecajun, Steve Riley and the Mamou Playboys, and Feufollet, just to name a few.

The crowd grows and the folding chairs pop out. You watch from the sidelines at the seasoned dancers who never tire from the infectious music of Acadien ancestry. When the bands change, meander on over to the Bayou Food Festival.

Under live oaks hanging like a velvet curtain, the smells draw you to the booths and the beer. Seafood lasagna, crawfish beignets, fried crab cake with crab sauce, homemade boudin, sweet potato pie, and much more. The area's best restaurants and caterers show their stuff with a flourish.

But wait, there's two more music stages. The Heritage Pavilion features an informal workshop and performance stage by the best in Cajun and Creole artists. You can bring your own instrument and sit in at the Louisiana Folk Roots Tent.

The Louisiana Crafts Festival joined the fun in 2002, offering lots of demonstrating and selling from traditional and fine artists and craftspeople.

La Vie Cadienne Wetlands & Folklife Festival adds a whole new dimension to the Cajun Fest. At Girard Park Lake, meet hunters, fishermen, shrimpers, craftsmen, and wetland specialists as they share their know-how, skills and tall tales. It's not just the music and the food that make up the Acadien people.

Ready to dance? Sure you are, cher! By now, the contagious attitude has rubbed off on you. Grab your partner (or pick one from the crowd) and kick up a little Cajun dust.

Festivals Acadiens runs Saturday and Sunday at Girard Park, but it actually begins Friday night with Downtown Alive!, Lafayette's premier TGIF party. The party starts at noon with music in Parc de Lafayette and continues into the night with a fais do-do street dance. Kids Alive! provides more music plus hands-on activities for les petite enfants.

If you've got a little time Sunday morning before the third day of festivities, drive down to New Iberia. When you're as big a James Lee Burke fan as I am, being in the same town as Dave Robicheaux and his creator is a real thrill. Eight foot stalks of sugarcane blow in the fields just off the road. The Bayou Teche rolls slowly by The Shadows, a tourist mecca replete with Cajun ghosts aplenty. Scenes Burke describes in his books come vividly to life in this magical little town just down from Avery Island, home of Tabasco.

It's time to head back to "the heart of French Louisiana." The final day of Festivals Acadiens is kicking off in the park at 11:00 AM. It's time to try (or resample) all the food you missed on Saturday and kick up some more dust over at the bandstand.

How does this all tie in to the Big Easy? Think Tipitina's on a Sunday afternoon. From 5:00-9:00 PM, Tip's at 501 Napoleon, features a Cajun fais do-do with Bruce Daigrepont. It recreates the dancehalls of Lafayette pretty well and the atmosphere is just as addictive. Mulate's at 201 Julia Street takes a hint from its Cajun cousin in Lafayette with fabulous food and dancing nightly. Michaul's, 840 St. Charles, and Patout's Cajun Cabin on Bourbon add a little extra spice to the musical merriment of the Crescent City.

When it comes to Louisiana's Cajun musical tapestry, it's all relative. And highly addictive.

For more info on Festivals Acadiens, call the Lafayette Convention and Visitors Commission, 1-800-346-1958 or log on CAJUNHOT.COM.

*King Kong gets beaded at the Bacchus parade*

# Make Mine Muses

In June of 2000, a unique thing happened in the world of Carnival. A krewe was formed; an all-woman's krewe that transcended race, age, socio-economic background, and position in the workforce. A female krewe devoid of king or queen; merely the goal of having more fun than humanly possible the Wednesday night before Mardi Gras.

Big Easy transplant Staci Rosenberg was on the street corner viewing the Druids parade one cold February night. Staci decided she, too, would like to ride and throw and be adored by the teeming masses of onlookers. The young attorney wasn't a member of one of New Orleans' elite old families, nor did she have an existing preference of krewes to pursue.

So she invented one.

Rosenberg contacted other "like-minded women" with a modern, creative kick for a krewe. Their name sprang from the nine legendary daughters of Zeus and Mnemosyne, and those streets that line the lower Garden District. Membership was affordable. The only requirement was that ladies be at least 18.

The call went out and was overwhelmingly answered. Doctors, lawyers, homemakers, teachers, TV personalities, waitresses, students, debutantes; women of diversity with a common goal: major league fun!

Thus was born the Krewe Of Muses. The gals' 21-float inaugural parade was positioned the Wednesday night before Fat Tuesday, February 21, 2001, along the traditional St. Charles route. Bead freaks were taken by surprise. Krewes come and go, all pomp and circumstance and old-line tradition. But the Muses brought forth a fount of guilty pleasures that crowds of onlookers adored. Greek-clad girls in wild abandon featuring music of The Wild Magnolias, Coolbone, The Executive Steel Band, Mo'Lasses (an all-woman brass band), plus an all-chick punk band (The Pink Slips) and the Shim Shamettes (a local burlesque group) broke the mold and secured a solid spot for this spanking new all-ladies parade.

605 riders took spots in their virgin romp, "Muses First." In 2002, 630 ladies mounted fabulous floats for "Muses Reaches The Terrible Two's." That same year, *Gambit Weekly* readers voted the krewe of Muses Best Overall Parade, Best Night Parade, and Favorite Theme. The Muses were the only parade to receive Five Crowns.

As in a mythological tale, this diverse and spunky group of ladies was the talk of Carnival.

Throws became collector's items. Designer Evelyn Menge used the likeness of New Orleans' famous street tile lettering to create the Muses' logo beads. A high-heeled medallion necklace changes each year to mark the heights of fashion. Bead purses, leaf medallion necklaces, light-up blinking beads and dangling lipstick medallion beads are just the beginning of the Muses' colorful and keepable tossouts.

Contests held among local high school artists determine each year's cup design. Community involvement continues with floats, designed by Kern International staff and customized by area artists. A contest for best costume and headpiece design is also on the agenda. There's even a Police Appreciation Luncheon for those hardworking troops who keep the crowds under control.

Each year, a different muse is featured as the parade's theme. In 2002, Clio, muse of history, brought forth millenniums of historical float ideas. Local Mardi Gras historian and teacher, Cherice Harrison-Nelson, was honorary Clio. Terpsichore, muse of the dance, was spotlighted in 2003. The Muses' theme is always a secret, well-guarded until parade night.

Though interest grows daily, the Muses don't intend to become a superkrewe. Captain and co-founder Staci Rosenberg wants to keep it "small and hands-on." Riders won't balloon past 700. There's a waiting list for "non-riders," in case members become with child or decide not to ride. But I'm told it's almost as long as the riders list.

Care to join, ladies? Even if you're not a N'awlins resident, you can enlist as a non-rider of Muses. It's only $100, and you receive all the benefits of riders, except the parade. That includes newsletters, other communications, and meetings, plus the Twelfth Night Party, Float Viewing Party, Pre-Parade and After-Parade Party and others. Outings are extra, but you pay the same as riding members.

Now the "keep-your-fingers-crossed" part. In early June, after the deadline for existing members to pay their dues, the Muses decide how many riding members will be chosen. There's no internal clout; a spot opens to the next person on the list. If you're picked from the non-riders-in-waiting, you get an invitation by mail. The cost goes up considerably for initiation fee, krewe throws, and more (and you have to spend up to $500 extra in beads). But compared to most krewes (especially Bacchus and Endymion), the cost is worth the ride of a lifetime.

There's even been discussion of a scholarship to help out those not able to meet the financial requirements.

"In addition to celebrating the spirit of being a Muse," Captain Rosenberg states, "our vision is to tap into the local artistic and cultural resources of our community and incorporate them into the Muses Mardi Gras tradition, making the whole community part of our parade."

To find out more about Calliope, Clio, Erato, Euterpe, Melpomene, Polymnia, Terpsichore, Thalia and Urania, log on to KREWEOFMUSES.ORG.

Their theme says it all: "In the celebration of Mardi Gras, the strength of womanhood and the spirit of New Orleans…happy are those whom the Muses love."

# §3
# *Historical References*

# Wedding In Wax

WE NEVER THOUGHT they'd do it. We especially never thought they'd do it where they did it.

Ritchie and Heather had been dating forever, it seemed. They'd been through the height of Anne Rice's Vampire Lestat Fan Club, where Ritchie was president, the man of the hour. They'd seen the club as it fizzled into a Lestat-induced coma, ready to retreat underground for a few decades.

Ritchie finally gave up the helm. It saddened him a great deal, after all the work he'd put into the club. He went full-bore into finishing his degree in computer graphics.

But he and Heather stayed the course.

I saw him in late February of 2002, while I was doing a booksigning in Metairie. Ritchie was the only soul I knew at the mall, let alone all of Metairie. Talk about a friend in need. He stayed almost the whole two hours; even bought copies of *Big Easy Dreamin'* for his sister Julie and for Chris and Karen, members of the rock band Peabody.

That's when Ritchie gave me the news. He and Heather were finally getting hitched! The wedding was set for early April, a week before French Quarter Festival. "You could've timed it for the fest, dude," I laughed.

But then, he'd never've been able to get a hotel room, not to mention the site. The Champagne-Scully wedding would take place at the Musee Conti. The friggin' wax museum, of all places!

Heather had gotten the idea in a local bride's magazine. It proclaimed, "give them a wedding they'll never forget. Get waxed."

"When we walked into the Musee Conti, it resembled the Green Velvet Ballroom at St. Elizabeth's (Anne Rice's property), except no green velvet," said Heather. "It had almost the same feel. We loved the French Quarter Room overlooking the street onto the Vieux Carre. And the best part was that there was an old museum filled with wax sculptures along with a history lesson of New Orleans. Just a really cool place to get our lives started."

Ritchie handed me an invitation he'd crafted, a gorgeous shot he'd taken of St. Louis Cathedral at sunset. Ritchie's also a great photographer; does a lot of concerts for hire. Took some splendid shots at the Anne Rice gatherings alongside Steve Patrick and myself.

How could I refuse? Besides, no one would ever believe me when I told them where it was gonna be.

Brenda, Sean and I secured a room at the Ramada Inn on Gravier Street in the Central Business District (CBD). Not the closest hotel to the Quarter, but the price (and parking) were pretty decent for in-season rates.

After a day of walking and shopping in the Vieux Carre, we showered and rested, then dude-ed up and (sensibly) took a cab to 917 Conti Street, a half block off Dauphine, to "the wax museum of Louisiana legends." I began to wonder if we'd be nestled among waxen historical figures as the nuptials began. That's when kindly ushers sent us up a flight of steps.

Chairs were already filling to capacity with family and friends as we crested the staircase. Since I'd decided to be an unpaid cameraman as my wedding gift, I began lurking in back rooms, in search of the reclusively separate bride and groom.

Only Ritchie's eyes gave away his nerves. Otherwise, he was the ringmaster as always, charming in his black tux. I caught several shots of the groom and his entourage near one of the bathrooms.

Heather was making final preps on her bridal gown, attendants at the ready. I was taken with the charming antiquity of the building, its exposed beams and high ceilings. The New Orleans Wax Museum (Musee Conti) was founded in 1963; family owned and operated into the third generation. Over 300 years of Louisiana and New Orleans history is represented in 154 life-size wax figures in "historically accurate settings."

I couldn't wait to see LaSalle alongside native Americans; the discovery of the mouth of the Mississippi River and the claiming of the territory for France. Or the Ursuline "casket girls" arriving in the city, keelboats in the background. Or Governor O'Reilly executing revolutionaries that had kicked out the first Spanish governor. Or even a voodoo priestess with accompanying python.

But all that would have to wait. There was a wedding to attend upstairs.

Ritchie and Heather's ceremony was one of the sweetest I've seen in recent years. As folding chairs were moved to accommodate tables for the guests, I began snapping shots for the couple's scrapbook: Ritchie dancing with his mom; our son Sean having his first sip of champagne with the newlyweds; the groom's cake, done up in a brown and white checkerboard pattern from an old Cheap Trick album; the bride's cake, complete with pulls for the unwed ladies to predict their future; a very pregnant Julie Champagne Abadie beaming at her brother; the bride and groom cake feedings and toast, the bouquet toss; the garter belt toss; and my favorite, Ritchie and Heather second-lining through the banquet room, umbrella in tow.

Food and drink were delicious and plentiful. A DJ provided many of the couples' favorite tunes. Imbibed spirits mingled freely with the spirits of the Musee Conti, inviting us all downstairs.

It was time to tour the wax museum!

Our friends Deb and Keith joined us in the narrow hallway, leading through a waxen Crescent City history tour. Keith, an experienced and animated tour guide, came alive, elaborating scenes for the ever-growing crowd. He was in his element, documenting James Monroe and Robert Livingston negotiating with a bathing Napoleon for the Louisiana Purchase in 1803. Keith regaled us with the horrors of Madame Lalaurie, how she tortured her servants in the attic of her French Quarter home. The Baroness Pontalba gave a stern command over the construction of her apartments in Jackson Square. Marie Laveau presided over a voodoo ritual. A group of Italians were executed after murdering New Orleans' first police chief. A waxen Mardi Gras Indian ruffled his feathers. Former Governor Edwin Edwards invited us into The Haunted Dungeon, where Dracula held court.

"There he goes again," laughed Deb, as her talkative husband regaled the wedding party. Ritchie and Heather had their picture made in front of Andy Jackson amidst the Battle Of New Orleans.

The reception went on well into the night. When it was time to say adieu, we all gathered outside. Ritchie and Heather dashed through the double doors amid a shower of bubbles blown by the attendees. I snapped a lone photo: a parting shot of the newlyweds smiling out the back window of their limo, eyes glazed and happy, rolling off into their new future.

"You know, I picked up more issues of that local bride magazine and saw no mention of the Wax Museum," recalls Heather. "It was truly meant to be for the two of us. I'm really glad it made an impression on our guests the same as it did for us, first setting eyes on the place."

Next time you're in The Big Easy, you don't have to get married to visit the Musee Conti, "a New Orleans treasure chest of history, legend and scandal." Besides the regular tour (open to corporate and school groups), the Museum offers a Voodoo Tour (complete with special love potion drink), seated dinners, cocktail receptions, parades, theme parties, and of course, wax weddings.

Log on WWW.GET-WAXED.COM for the full story.

# Train-ing Day

MY WIFE AND SON will be the first to tell you the coolest method of travel to Mardi Gras is via the infamous train, The City Of New Orleans. Brenda presented me with her plan a few weeks before Fat Tuesday. Amtrak was offering a buy one-get one ticket special from Jackson to New Orleans. Kids rode half price. How 'bout, Brenda said, if she and Sean took the train down and I drove the car. They could head back on Sunday in time for school in Brenda's Saturn and I'd ride the City Of New Orleans home on Ash Wednesday.

I knew there had to be a catch. They got to have all the fun.

"Hurry up and wait" was the evident catchphrase at the train station in downtown Jackson, Mississippi. Heavy construction for a world class transportation dock made it look more like a bombed out third world village. After what seemed like hours, the southbound train pulled up, and the tired, eager crowd began stepping over boards and debris to enter.

Adding to the Carnival bound confusion, assigned seating wasn't regulated. It was sit-as-sit-can. Brenda and a purple, gold and green clad Sean quickly discovered the majority of riders were camped out in the entertainment car. A raucous brass band served as backdrop to wide swivel chairs, a glass ceiling and cash bar. City Of New Orleans medallion beads were being handed out like candy along with other throws.

The party was already in progress and had been brewing as far north as Chicago the day before. A few people trickled off the City Of New Orleans at various small-town stops. But the train was taking on more and more guests, eagerly anticipating the parades and debauchery ahead.

"We toured every inch of the train," Brenda said. "Upstairs and down, from the front sleeping cars to the rear dinner car."

"I liked going from one car to the next to the next," beamed Sean. Watching the tracks pass beneath his feet was as frightening to the eight year old as it was exhilarating. He even managed to stumble onto the sleeping car and ruffle a few snoozers. (Sleeping during a party? What's wrong with them?)

Sean and mom purchased assorted snacks and fast food, then settled in for the ride.

"Excited chatter was everywhere," Brenda recalls. "The first question was always, 'Where did you get on?'"

Everyone had a Mardi Gras adventure they wanted to share. It was obvious many guests made this an annual excursion. They carried ice chests and travel gear that resembled a campout. Their virgin train-ing day had been years ago.

The entertainment car continued to belt out Carnival tunes. Two bands played back to back, gladly accepting tips to be used as spending money in the Big Easy. Brenda strongly suspected the bands' train ride (as well as their drinks) was payment for their musical merriment.

So where was I? Most likely, sitting in bumper to bumper traffic on I-10, starting from Kenner to the St. Charles Avenue exit. It was inevitable, so I just turned up the radio and crept along.

I arrived at the Garden District Bookshop on Prytania about fifteen minutes before Brenda and Sean's cab pulled up. Our friend, Deb, is the manager there and we were staying with her and husband Keith. You can imagine the difference in our demeanors: the husband who'd been driving for nearly four hours and the wife and kid with the train-induced Mardi Gras buzz.

"The cabbies weren't at all interested in going to the French Quarter," Brenda recalls. "So we were glad to be heading in the opposite direction." Brenda suggests if you're de-training and ready to brave the Quarter, ask a cab to take you to St. Charles Avenue and catch a streetcar to Canal Street. It's only an extra buck and a quarter. Holding up a sign to alert cabs of your destination can also save time and frustration.

The first passenger train from The Windy City to the Crescent City began in 1873. It took almost fifty hours to travel the 912 mile Chicago to New Orleans route. The route's importance grew in 1912 when the Illinois Central Railroad commemorated the opening of the Panama Canal. The Panama Limited debuted on December 1 of that year.

The City Of New Orleans rolled on April 27, 1947, providing basic transportation for the largely rural market along its route.

In the "halcyon days" of train travel, the daytime City Of New Orleans and the overnight Panama Limited kept a sixteen hour or less schedule from Chicago to New Orleans. The two trains originally offered an on-board stewardess, connecting coaches from Louisville and St. Louis, full dining service and a radio-equipped observation lounge.

The City Of New Orleans was discontinued in the early 1960's. But due to the popularity of Arlo Guthrie's train song of the same name, The Panama Limited was given the handle of its sister.

Illinois Central joined Amtrak on April 30, 1971, since the City Of New Orleans' costs were lower and ridership more robust. The superliner arrived in 1994, with three Genesis P42 units pulling its passenger load. An all-sleeper Mardi Gras "party train" debuted as an extra section from Chicago in 1996. And the rest is Mardi Gras history.

Take it from Brenda and Sean, who had the ride of their lives on the liveliest train to coast the carnival tracks to Mardi Gras. Kick back, watch the tiny towns zip by, and live it up on your appetizer to Carnival: The City Of New Orleans.

# Rollin' On The River

THEY REST IN the muddy currents like mammoth party favors. Tourists trickle across the boarding plank like ants onto a cake, eagerly awaiting the roll of the paddle wheel, the billow of smoke and the timeless tunes from the calliope.

They've stepped into the past for a two hour tour 'cross the Mississippi River, under the Crescent City Connection, past the Aquarium and Riverwalk. Wide-eyed and smiling after a few Hurricanes and Dixie longnecks, these madras and khaki covered visitors are privy to a history over two hundred years in the making.

The Natchez, the John James Audubon, the Creole Queen, and the Cajun Queen are regulars on the Crescent City waterfront, ridden and enjoyed by millions. But let's turn the clock back to the late seventeen hundreds, to the real reason these majestic ships were created and why they still harbor a romantic tug on our heartstrings.

In the early days of commerce, Americans depended on the rivers to ship their produce to foreign markets. Primitively fabricated flatboats, keelboats and rafts carried grain, whiskey, cattle, lead, salt, and furs down to New Orleans from ports upriver. Without an engine to push against the tide, most boats never made a return trip. Their riders, a hearty lot, either walked or rode horses back home via the Natchez Trace.

When the river fell and the flatboats were stranded, they were either burned or broken up for lumber. Many stores, taverns and boarding houses sprang up from a previous life as flatboats and keelboats.

It was time for improved river transportation. The first Mississippi River steamboat, "The New Orleans," was launched on January 10, 1812, from plans by Robert G.C. Fee, a naval architect. "The waterfront was crowded with the curious; even the territorial legislature had to be recessed so that its members could see this new wonder that Governor Claiborne claimed would make New Orleans one of the great cities of the world."

"The New Orleans" was 148 feet long, with a 20 foot beam. "Her bowsprit and her two masts with sails unfurled, and her long sleek cabins outlined by portholes were in the best maritime tradition." It cost the owners—The Mississippi Steamboat Navigation Company—$38,000 to build. Robert Fulton and Robert Livingston were among the company's founders.

Running time for the 2,000 mile trip from Pittsburgh to New Orleans was 259 hours, an average of eight miles per hour.

Steamboat commerce and travel wasn't an overnight success. But by 1820, the Fulton-Livingston monopoly was overcome by faster, more practical boats. "Hulls were made shallower, with boilers and engines on the main deck, and a second deck was added for passengers."

The first steamship in coastal trade from New York to New Orleans was the "Robert Fulton." Constructed in 1820, it was 158 feet long.

Between 1830-40, 729 steamboats were built. The largest steamboat afloat was "The Ohio," built in 1849. It measured 267 feet, with a 46 foot beam, a 29 foot depth and weighed 2,434 tons. With 2,700-horsepower engines, "The Ohio" cost nearly $450,000 to build.

By 1854, the port of New Orleans brought forth "the busy hum of labor, voices of every tongue and people of every nation." It had truly become a hub of international trade. The levee was a busy place with peddlers, beggars, women food sellers and thieves.

Fire was a constant hazard among steamboats. With their wood construction and highly flammable cargo, these floating behemoths became deathtraps. And since boats were so numerous and moored close together, a fire would spread from one deck to another until several steamboats were ablaze.

By 1850, the Mississippi River steamboat had reached the "apex of design." In a forty year period between 1840 and 1880, more than 4,800 were put upon the waters. Bigger and more decorative boats were seen, upgraded into beautiful, majestic pieces of architecture.

From 1856-60, 4,800 steamboats arrived in New Orleans. River trade for those four years was $289 million; ocean commerce was $183 million.

The Civil War caused an almost complete halt to commercial steamboat traffic on the Mississippi River. Confederates destroyed boats to avoid capture or they were sunk in battle. There was a temporary post-war spurt of riverboat traffic, but the advent of the railroad system began to slowly turn the tide.

A famous Currier and Ives print depicts the Great Steamboat Race of 1870 between the Natchez and the Robert E. Lee. One-time partners, now rival captains, John Cannon (The Robert E. Lee, built in 1866) challenged T. P. Leathers of The Natchez (1869) to a race from New Orleans to St. Louis. The men even published "cards" in the daily papers on the day of the race disclaiming such a contest.

Cannon stripped the Lee down and carried no passengers; it was even refueled at midstream. Leathers was so overconfident of his sleek machine, he took freight and passengers on the Natchez. Big mistake.

The Robert E. Lee broke the New Orleans-St. Louis record in three days, eighteen hours and thirteen minutes. It was never bested by another steamboat.

In the 1880's many steamboats advertised in the *Daily Picayune* for travel to Cincinnati, Louisville, Memphis, Vicksburg and Natchez, among other destinations. These larger "floating palaces" were equipped with chandeliers, carved furniture, paintings, carpets and grand pianos.

Much freight was still being transported by river in 1895, but more and more boats were beginning to dock, never to return. By 1909, the St. Louis-Memphis-New Orleans packet lines were no more. River commerce was dying fast.

In October, 1862, after the fall of New Orleans in the Civil War, the Cromwell, New York and New Orleans Steamship Line began operations. Steamships ran directly to Europe, run by French, German and English shipping interests vying for the cotton trade. Huge and heavy barges pushed by towboats eventually replaced the steamboats, operating the Mississippi, Missouri and Ohio rivers.

The twentieth century led the way for larger, more powerful ships. New Orleans harbor was reconverted into a wider, safer passage for these mammoth tankers and cruise lines. Cargo ships from over forty nations arrive in the Port Of New Orleans annually. But visitors and locals can step back in time any day of the week and reminisce.

The paddle-wheeler Creole Queen and riverboat Cajun Queen have daily battlefield cruises, harbor cruises and dinner jazz cruises, not to mention charters, private parties and even weddings. The steamboat Natchez offers a two hour cruise and the John James Audubon is famous for its seven mile Aquarium to Zoo cruise.

Grab a brochure at the riverfront kiosk next to the Jax Brewery shopping center and take your pick. Just like the venerable streetcar, New Orleans' riverboats and steamboats give The Big Easy a fun and flavorful edge while respecting its historic aspect of travel and commerce.

# The Baroness

WHEN MOST TOURISTS saunter down Decatur Street taking in the ambiance of Jackson Square, St. Louis Cathedral, the Cabildo and the Presbytere, they pay little mind to the stately red brick buildings flanking these historically drenched places. Visitors sit under green and white striped canopies at the Café du Monde, sipping café au lait, brushing confectioners sugar off their laps and mustaches from just-devoured beignets. Locals gather at Christmastime for Carols in the Square. The World's Largest Jazz Brunch is held within this same space during French Quarter Fest in April.

Poised like beacons framed in ancient oaks, encasing restaurants, art galleries, and the State Tourism Information Center, rest the famous Pontalba Apartments. One of the most coveted living quarters in the Quarter, the classy, three story Pontalba Buildings that line St. Peter and St. Ann Streets were commissioned in 1850 by Baroness Micaela Almonester Pontalba.

The Baroness is one of the most colorful figures in New Orleans history. Mystery author Julie Smith even named one of her protagonists in honor of this legendary lady. Micaela Almonester was born in 1795, the daughter of Don Andres Almonester y Roxas. Don Andres arrived in the Crescent City in 1769 as a clerk. Eventually he would become one of the city's most wealthy and influential philanthropists

Now here's where the story gets interesting, in fine soap opera

fashion. Micaela was married at the age of sixteen to her distant cousin Celestin Pontalba. The wedding was held in the expansive St. Louis Cathedral. The couple then moved to Paris. During this period, young Micaela started getting bad vibes that her wedding had been a setup arranged by Celestin's father, the Baron Pontalba. You see, the new Mrs. Celestin Pontalba had a considerable dowry and inheritance: all the property squaring off the Place d'Armes. Prime real estate for a Baron with no scruples.

For over ten years, the trio fought over Micaela's money. Finally, the frustrated bride left her husband, their three kids in tow. The Baron quickly disinherited them. In 1834, when Micaela was thirty-nine, a violent encounter with her father-in-law ended with the Baron shooting Micaela four times in the chest. He then took his own life.

Micaela somehow managed to survive, losing two fingers in the scuffle. With the evil Baron out of the way, Micaela worked her way up to Baroness. Four years later, she divorced Celestin.

Europe was on the brink of revolution, prompting the Baroness and her brood to move back to New Orleans in 1849. Her prized real estate surrounding the Place d'Armes seemed rundown compared to the newer buildings across Canal Street in the American sector. The Baroness was ready to build. The influence of Paris architecture had rubbed off on Micaela; she hired famed architect James Gallier, Sr. to begin the project. Gallier is responsible for the Greek Revival colonnades seen on many of the Pontalba buildings. The large courtyards in the back together with commercial units on the ground floor and living quarters above are more Creole in origin.

According to the Rough Guide to New Orleans, the Baroness was a "harsh taskmistress, supervising construction to the last detail and refusing to pay for the many changes she demanded." It's OK, you can say it: Bitch!

After countless architectural arguments, Micaela ended up firing Gallier. Big surprise. She then hired Henry Howard to complete and build her famous dwellings.

Many claim the Pontalba Buildings were the first apartments in the U.S. Not true. But they were among the first to use mass produced materials like cast iron. The iron was cast in New York, the red brick pressed in Baltimore, and the plate glass and slate roofs were manufactured in England.

In 1851, the completed Pontalba Apartments cost a whopping $302,000. The final effect featured wide galleries and balconies sporting decorative curlicues centered on cast iron railings inscribed with the initials A&P: Almonester and Pontalba. The scrollwork was designed by the Baroness herself. New Orleans became hooked on the lacy cast iron, replacing the simple hand wrought iron fashioned by local slaves.

Renovations began in the square. In January, 1851, the city council changed the parade grounds' name from Place d'Armes to Jackson Square in honor of Andrew Jackson, the hero of the Battle of New Orleans. Interest stimulated by the Baroness' buildings prompted the Jackson Monument Association to raise funds for a statue. The Legislature kicked in $10,000 for the project. In 1856, Clark Miller's equestrian statue of Andy Jackson was unveiled. It still stands (on two back legs) today.

But the Baroness had already made other plans. Her ex had taken a turn for the worse. Micaela returned to Paris for a reconciliation. But you have to wonder. This shrewd businesswoman coerced a seriously ill Celestin to hand over his affairs to the Baroness, who added all his property to hers.

Meanwhile back in the Crescent City, Civil War had broken out. The Quarter declined and the Pontalba Apartments lost their luster.

The Baroness lasted a few years past the War Between the States. She died a rich and shrewd Paris matron at the age of seventy-nine, passing away in 1874. By the turn of the twentieth century, the once beautiful Pontalba Buildings became tenements. During one of the city's numerous yellow fever epidemics, a cow was reported inhabiting one of the Pontalba's rooms.

The Works Progress Administration (WPA) rode in to save the day. In the 1930's, the WPA began in earnest to renovate the once decimated Pontalba Buildings.

Today, the product of a woman who survived all odds and lived to seize power and control, surrounds two sides of Jackson Square like half a magnificent frame bordering the most famous picture in New Orleans. Perhaps Micaela Almonester Pontalba's demands were a bit on the dramatic side, but what a grand result of architecture.

The next time you're heading down Decatur, drinking a cool one, drink in the magnificence of the Pontalba Apartments. Dream of a Baroness whom neither bullets nor treachery could stop. And dream of living in one of the most desirable locales in all of the Big Easy.

# *Hoodoo*

WHENEVER I MENTION the word "voodoo" to anyone living outside of New Orleans, I get the same reaction: their eyes grow wide, their mouth forms into a small, pronounced "O", and they generally start gibbering in an unintelligible language meant to show their panic at being the focus of a possible "hex."

So I knew this essay would be one of the most eye-opening (and hopefully, educational) tidbits to be served under the auspices of these pages.

Most people I've asked didn't have a working knowledge of voodoo, its history, and current status in the Crescent City. They just seemed creeped-out at the mere thought of snakes and drums and rituals and gris-gris and all the red x's on Marie Laveau's tomb. Or maybe even Baron Samedi—the lord of the dead—rising out of his grave from "Live And Let Die," trying to keep James Bond from his appointed tarot reading with Jane Seymour's Solitaire.

Then I got to thinking: Voodoo is all about fear; fear of the unknown. Fear that someone has got your number all tied up in a fetish doll with stickpins at the ready. Voodoo is all about the power of the mind; in the belief that someone is controlling your destiny. Controlling it through the Loa—the spirit world. And right at this very moment, they're filling a gris-gris bag full of black cat bones, goofer dust, herbs, pepper and a coin or two. They're gonna put it on your doorstep tonight near midnight and POW! your life is ruined. Unless you get protection. And that costs money. You've gotta get a counter spell to break the curse.

So, where did all this fear come from and how far has it gone? In perhaps the best book on the subject, Robert Tallant's *Voodoo in New Orleans* (first published in 1946), Voodoo entered the states nearly three hundred years ago. Raids on the African Slave Coast began around 1724. These snake worshipping people were sold into the West Indies. The name of their snake-god was Vodu, which was corrupted into Voodoo, Voudou, Vaudau, Voudoux, or Vaudaux…and eventually, Hoodoo. The name not only included the god and the worshiping sect, but also the rites and practices, priests and priestesses, and those who followed its teachings.

Another possible origin suggests that followers of Frenchman Peter Valdo (the Waldenses or Vaudois) used witchcraft and human sacrifice, and early settlers carried it to the French West Indies. Voodoo spread like wildfire through the islands and then on to The Bayou State. In 1782, Louisiana's Governor Galvez banned the import of Negro slaves from Martinique because they "would make the lives of citizens unsafe." Within ten years, Negroes from Santo Domingo were likewise halted.

Under French and Spanish rule, the lives of Negro slaves in Louisiana were tainted with constant pain and misery. "Their only escape was in death." Fear of uprisings initiated by voodoo worshipers like those in Haiti kept the pressure on. Public meetings of slaves were out of the question. Plantation owners were even threatened with fines if gatherings should take place.

It wasn't until the Louisiana Purchase in 1803 that restrictions were lifted. Slave trade from the West Indies was again granted. This was the beginning of organized voodoo in Louisiana. Second and third generation Louisiana slaves were now beginning to meet island practitioners who were never forced to relinquish their religion.

The first organized voodoo gathering was said to be in an abandoned brickyard on Dumaine Street. They met late at night for their dancing, drinking, and eventually, orgies. The police soon got wind and the voodoos took their rituals to the water, meeting at the banks of Bayou St. John and Lake Pontchartrain. The king and queen reigned, fires blazed, drums beat, snakes took center stage, and animals were sacrificed, filling the sacred bowl with their blood. The queen raised a python up and let it kiss her cheek. She was inflamed with a *power* and passed it on to her followers through touch.

The voodoo god—the Zombie—was represented by a male dancer. He would dance around a great cauldron filled with offerings by members of the sect: frogs, chickens, snails, cats, and always a snake. The queen would chant: "L'appe vini, le grand Zombie, L'appe vini pou fe gris gris." This translated to "He is coming, the great Zombie, he is coming to make gris gris."

"Live chickens and pigeons were sometimes introduced to the rites, torn to pieces with the fingers and teeth of the dancers. They fell to the ground in embraces of frenzied lust. They were possessed. They had the *power*."

Sacrifice and blood drinking were integral parts of the voodoo ceremonies. The blood of a goat was usually used, but often it was a black cat. Sometimes a missing child was rumored to be the object of a sacrifice, a "goat without horns." Add to that the small ceremonial coffin carried by the Zombie dancer, and the populace was terrified.

One of the most famous voodoo practitioners was Doctor John. He was huge, a free man of color, and owned his own slaves. He claimed to be a Senagalese prince and carried the facial scars to prove it.

Doctor John had been a ship worker, finally ending up as a cotton roller on the docks of New Orleans. His size and purported voodoo *power* gained the Doctor notoriety and he was soon charging for his special services. John specialized in healing, selling gris-gris, and fortune telling. With his savings, Doctor John bought property on the Bayou Road and built a house. He purchased female slaves and married several.

Upper class white ladies sought out Doctor John's advice in the matters of love and vengeance. Unknown to his clients, the Doctor hired out many "agents" who worked as servants in the homes of these families. "Magical" information was always easy to get. It's said that Doctor John knew more about the prominent families of 1840's New Orleans than any other living person. When the upper crust sat in Doctor John's "odorous little house, surrounded by all the paraphernalia of the witch doctor's profession" and had all their innermost secrets described to them, they couldn't help but be impressed.

During this same era, an unassuming young woman named Marie would seize one opportunity after another to become the most powerful and revered voodooienne in history.

The first reliable record of Marie Laveau was her marriage to Jacques Paris on August 4, 1819 in the St. Louis Cathedral. She was the illegitimate daughter of Charles Laveau and Marguerite Darcantel; a mixture of African-American, Native American and white; described as "tall, statuesque, a woman with curling black hair, good features, dark skin that had a distinctly reddish cast and fierce black eyes."

Marie and Jacques were both free people of color. Both were Roman Catholic. Jacques was a carpenter. Marie was reputed to have aided victims during the Yellow Fever epidemics. She always prayed at the Cathedral in which she was married. The couple shared a house on the 1900 block of North Rampart, bestowed to Marie as a wedding gift by her father.

The Parises had been married only a short while when Jacques went missing, never to return. Marie was dubbed the "Widow Paris." To make ends meet, she became a hairdresser, styling the heads of prominent white and Creole women.

These women shared intimate secrets with their stylist; family skeletons Marie would file away and use at a later time to serve her "magical" needs. Only your voodoo priestess knows for sure.

Marie worked her magic with Doctor John for a time; she learned much in the art of chicanery from the giant voodoo priest. A shrewd businesswoman, Marie began to realize she could gain much more ground (and money) on her own. She took a lover, Christophe Glapion, and rose among the ranks of the voodoos. By 1830, Marie Laveau was a queen.

Marie began adding new dimensions to Haitian voodoo, both borrowed and original. Roman Catholic statues of saints, plus prayers, incense, and holy water began to merge with snakes, drums and animal sacrifice. Laveau renounced devil worship and insisted her followers were Christians. Rival queens were quickly dealt with, either by threats, powerful gris-gris, or personal beatings by Marie herself. She took charge of the Congo Square dances—the Sunday afternoon gatherings where Armstrong Park is today—where many say Jazz has its deepest roots. Voodoo rituals along the lake and bayou grew in size and popularity. Marie invited everyone to participate. Her control over New Orleans' black population was almost absolute.

During this same era, the voodoo queen acquired a new residence. Upon aiding a wealthy man's son in a murder trial through prayer and enchantments, the father presented Marie with a small cottage on Rue St. Ann between North Rampart and Burgundy. It was dubbed Maison Blanche (the white house). She lived there until her death in 1881.

In the 1850's the Widow Paris became interested in New Orleans' prison population. Marie was a well-known figure around the cells of men awaiting execution, bringing them gumbo, talk, and prayers. Her priorities were changing, but respect never wavered.

Around 1875, Marie Laveau performed her best spell yet, extending her life into a new generation. The Widow Paris would retire and a new Marie would walk the streets, even inhabit the same cottage. Marie Glapion, born February 2, 1827, had a remarkable resemblance to her mother. Marie I had borne fifteen children; some of them died, but many survived. The Maison Blanche was full of children, grandchildren, and a withered old Widow no one really paid attention to. The next generation of voodoos assumed Marie's eternal beauty was through the power of the Loa.

Marie Glapion was fifty-four and at the height of her career when her mother died. Marie II lived and reigned until 1897. Her body was placed atop the bones of the original voodoo queen, in a receiving vault in Lafayette Cemetery N° 1. Believers knock three times on the headstone and ask a favor. They bring flowers, burn candles, leave money and mark the grave with red x's for luck.

By the turn of the century, voodoo had changed and fallen into segments. The intervention of Marie Laveau and her daughter had given New Orleans a voodoo all its own, much of which still remains intact today.

Voodoo is big business in the Big Easy; fifteen percent of its population are practitioners. Tourists flock to the Historic Voodoo Museum (opened in 1972) at 724 Dumaine in the Quarter, for tours, gifts and the ever-present gris-gris bag to take home to friends. Rituals (complete with snakes) are held every St. John's Eve (June 23) and Halloween for paying customers. Marie Laveau's Voodoo Shop on Bourbon Street is another tourist grabber, offering fetish dolls, incense, intention herbs, beads, and even T-shirts.

Looking for something a bit less touristy? Check out the Voodoo

Spiritual Temple (VST) at 828 North Rampart. Established in 1990 by Priestess Miriam and Priest Oswan Chamani, the VST focuses on "traditional West African spiritual and herbal healing and practices currently in New Orleans." Since Chamani "transcended into the arms of the ancestors" in 1995, the temple is run by Priestess Miriam.

In an open web forum on the VST web site (www.VOODOOSPIRITUALTEMPLE.ORG), Louis Martinie answers contemporary questions concerning voodoo. "As a spiritual system, (voodoo) is continually evolving to serve a tremendously wide range of loa (spirits)," writes Martinie. "Each temple or spiritual house operates independently; this lends itself to wide variability in theory and practice."

Other characteristics of voodoo include offerings to the Marassa (twins), the Dead (ancestors), the loa (spirits), and an absolute god or goddess. Sacrifice in the form of animal, vegetable, mineral, liquid or a "subtle giving of the priest's or priestess' energy is offered to the loa. Possession, full or partial, is very common."

A voodoo ceremony usually offers services to the three elements mentioned above. "A Gate Opener (Papa La Ba, Papa Legba, Ellegua) will be petitioned to open the gate between the Visible and Invisible Worlds. A sacrifice will be offered. Living snakes are often in the ceremonies."

"In the end," writes Martinie, "Voodoo is experimental; if you would know its essence, ask the loa…they provide the most direct answers."

Smoke and mirrors or power of the mind? It all depends on what you choose to believe. But believe this: Doctor John and Marie Laveau forever changed voodoo in New Orleans. Today, they're celebrated as two of the main loa in the City That Care Forgot.

I guess it all depends on who you know…and the secrets you've learned about them; whether you've extracted their skeletons as a hairdresser, a witch doctor, or a purveyor of the gossip mill. Some see voodoo as a tent show designed to bilk the currency of curious onlookers. Others channel fear from lack of knowledge and the over-dramatization from TV and movies. Still others believe in voodoo's spirituality and the purposes it serves through prayer and homage to the spirit world.

So next time someone mentions voodoo in your presence, don't panic. Forget what you thought you knew. Now you know the truth.

And don't let that little doll sitting on your doorstep worry you one bit…

# Makin' Groceries

AN OLD ADAGE commonly used in the Big Easy in years past was, "makin' groceries." I've always enjoyed using that expression in lieu of, "I'm heading off to the grocery store." The term originated over two hundred years ago near the banks of the mighty Mississippi at a certain market where tourists and locals thrive. They called this weekly food necessity "makin' market."

Makin' groceries in New Orleans began in earnest in 1791 at the present site of today's French Market on lower Decatur Street near the Mint. Spanish authorities erected a building that year called La Hall des Boucheries. For nineteen years, the Spanish Market supplied much of the meat, poultry and vegetables to the citizens of New Orleans. La Hall des Boucheries was destroyed in 1812. That same year, an arcaded structure designed by city surveyor Jacques Tanesse was built in the original market spot.

A melting pot of citizenry crowded the market as early as 3:00 AM. By 9:00, it was almost deserted. English, French, Spanish, Irish, Italian, African American, German, and other nationalities converged to "make market." Choctaw Indian squaws near Bayou Lacombe in St. Tammany Parish across Lake Pontchartrain sold herbs, roots and file (dried sassafras used in gumbo); they also made and sold baskets.

Parts of a vegetable market were added in 1823, extending from Dumaine to St. Phillip Streets. The market house held more than one hundred stalls. It was three hundred feet long and cost $30,000. "

"Its low-pitched tile roof and arcaded sides made it an impressive building," quotes *New Orleans—A Pictorial History*, "(It was) particularly thrilling to those approaching by water." The French market was "an object of curiosity" to every visitor.

Peddling was the first step above a laborer's job. But it was a proud occupation for those with the knack to grow, make and sell their specialties. A common sight on the riverfront market was the Cala Woman. Calas are coarse rice fritters made of flour, eggs, butter, milk, sugar, boiled head rice and yeast, sponge-mixed into a stiff batter. The fritters are then formed by dropping spoonfuls of the batter into deep hot fat. Reminds me of drop biscuits. The Cala women carried baskets of their goodies perched atop their heads, selling them early in the morning for breakfast. Other "basket heads" included the Vegetable Lady, the Blackberry Woman and the Praline Mammy, who sold brown pecan and pink or white coconut pralines from her basket. Renderings of these famous peddlers can still be found in the French Market of today.

The American side of Canal Street began to clamor for its own market. So in 1838, the Poydras Market was erected in the middle of Poydras Street between Baronne and South Rampart. The Poydras Market flourished for almost a hundred years until it was demolished in 1930. That same period saw a rebirth of the original French Market under the WPA, the same folks who restored the Pontalba Buildings.

Today, the Farmers Market stalls in the 1100 block of North Peters are filled with the same fruits and vegetables peddled by their ancestors. Garlic and red peppers hang in strands from the rafters. Bananas, grapes, apples, and kumquats are stacked in wooden bins alongside sacks of beans and nuts. Cans of famous N'awlins coffee tempt your olfactory senses. A sea of pumpkins surround you in October. "Who's next?" shouts a merchant, anxious to bag your selection.

Further down, shelves of cookbooks, hot sauce, and Cajun seasonings vie for your attention. It's almost time to wet your whistle with bottled water, soft drinks or a sno-ball. Step right up to some alligator sausage and boiled crawfish at the seafood market. And yes, convenient bathrooms are nearby.

Now, you're beginning to enter the sea of beads and T-shirts. Food market turns to flea market. You're in the 1200 block of St. Peters.

Some shoppers turn back, but most press on, eager to check out the latest jewelry, sunglasses, custom lighters, incense burners, ceramic masks, African artifacts, New Orleans music and artistic prints, Mardi Gras boxer shorts and ties, woodcarvings, and tourist level voodoo. The Farmers and Flea Market is often packed like Creole sardines, but no one ever seems to mind. It's just plain fun for adults and kids alike. Mind that baby carriage!

I can imagine what things would've been like over two hundred years ago, when folks were makin' groceries down here near the riverfront. The hectic flow of selling and buying, the constant rush of commerce; the noise, the smells, the utter excitement.

Things haven't changed much in two centuries. Shoppers still know the best place to make groceries. For the freshest fruits and veggies, the hottest spices, the coolest gifts, and one of the most enjoyable enclosed strolls you'll have in the Crescent City, check out the French Market. We makin' groceries, dawlin'.

*Chartres Street Chimp*

# Street Talk

New Orleans' streets have as entertaining a history as the city itself. When you understand where, when and why these avenues, highways and byways, alleys and thoroughfares obtained their unique appellations, you perceive the Big Easy from a more intimate level: street level.

Author and cartoonist John Chase released a dandy book in 1946 called *Frenchmen, Desire, Good Children*. The title was derived from three avenues in the city. In his humorous methodology, both artful and prose-hearty, Chase did extensive research into the naming of New Orleans' streets. I've managed, if only meagerly, to cull a ripe selection of Chase's results. But it still only scratches the surface.

Ready? Let's hit the streets!

With an original mixture of French Bourbon-Orleans, later spiced with chunks of Choctaw Indian and generous portions of Spanish, the streets of the city named for the second Phillip, Duke of Orleans, were ripe for name-calling. In 1718, Jean Baptiste La Moyne, Sieur de Bienville, crowned New Orleans the capital of Louisiana. Three years later, the city's engineer, Adrian de Pauger, was charged with designing "a classical, symmetrical gridiron pattern" for the new town. But a Scotsman named John Law ordered the names of the premiere streets.

Law was a gambler by profession, the alleged inventor of inflation and credit in Louisiana. He created a system called the Mississippi

Company and a bank that issued the first paper currency in the new land. Law needed immigrants to become citizens of his town. He engaged a recruiter to bring in, firstly, contraband salt dealers, then ex-convicts and beggars. Law commissioned de Pauger to knight the town Neuvelle (New) Orleans with French-accented streets. "It must be established in the minds of everybody that this was a crown colony." There were to be no Indian names. Law called for a church, an administration building, a governor's mansion, two barracks for the soldiers, a prison, and a general store.

Iberville and Bienville were the town's founding brothers. For their discovery in 1699, they got the first two streets. The duke of Bourbon was one of the bank's best customers. Let's name a street after him. Louis was a favored baptismal name for the Bourbons; it was also the king's name. Let's please the clergy and dub a street Rue Saint Louis. The House Of Orleans often baptized under the name Phillip. St. Phillip Street was born. A popular aristocratic name for the ladies was Ann. Women of the court are bank customers, too. Rue St. Ann sounds nice.

Noble families of Conti, Conde, Vendome and Chartres trace back to kissing cousins of the Bourbon-Orleans dynasty. Some of the first streets were named after them. Vendome was an earlier name for Dauphine Street. Until 1865, the section of Rue Chartres from Jackson Square to Esplanade was called Conde.

The king's father was the Duke of Burgundy; there's a street named after him. The Compte de Toulouse was important in the Navy; a street and a Doobie Brothers album came from that guy. Remember the barracks John Law asked to be erected for the troops stationed in the provinces? There's a Barracks Street in the lower Quarter.

As a gambler, Law was real loser, especially when it came to the bold new French city. Instead of wiping out the deficit of King Louis XIV, Law and the Duke of Orleans doubled it in only four years. Law died in 1729, "impoverished as the nation he had seduced."

But there were new neighborhoods forming and new streets to be named.

Probably the most tongue-twisting, spelling-impaired street in all of New Orleans is Tchoupitoulas. Legend has it a Frenchman came upon an Indian fishing. He asked the Native American how the fish were biting. The Indian replied in French, "Choupic ques tous la." The choupics (mudfish) were all there. Subsequently, the bayou and Indians living nearby were known as Tchoupitoulas (mud fish people). A more primitive form is Chapitoulas. That's Choctaw for "those who reside at the river."

Certain streets nabbed their names depending on their locations or association in the community. Rue de la Quai was French for Levee Street. That was its name until 1870 when the Mississippi River altered its course and New Orleans was no longer on a levee. The street is now called Decatur, after an honored naval officer. New Levee Street was changed to Peters, from Samuel J. Peters, father of the 2$^{nd}$ Municipality.

The road where Ursuline nuns built their first convent was originally named Saint Adrian after the town's engineer, Adrain de Pauger. The name changed to St. Ursala, then to Ursulines Street in honor of the nuns and their historic building. Not to be forgotten, there is a Pauger Street.

There was once an Arsenal Street in the lower Quarter, named for the nearby arsenal. Its name changed to Hospital Street for 180 years. The road is known today as Governor Nicholls, from the civil war hero who later became governor.

Kerlerec Street is designated after a famed naval officer. Kerlerec was an unskilled administrator; even the Indians had no respect for him. They called Kerlerec "Chef Menteur," meaning Chief (or big) Liar. Chef Menteur Highway runs through New Orleans East. That's right: Big Liar Highway.

In 1763, the Spanish acquired New Orleans and new roads were christened for Spanish governors: Galvez, Miro, Carondelet. The "grand avenue" bordering the Quarter was dubbed Esplanade.

A French revolt in 1768 produced several thoroughfares. The opposing Spaniards were led by Captain Jacinto Panis. Today's Jackson Avenue was originally Grand Avenue Panis. Bernard Marigny, who owned land that later became the Faubourg (suburb) Marigny, named more streets than any other man. Thirty-six years after the French revolutionists were executed, he called the bloody street Frenchman. Among his numerous street titles, Marigny dreamed of a heavenly thoroughfare. He designated one Champs Elysees. We know it as Elysian Fields. Other Marigny roads include Union, Bagatelle, Antoine, Peace, and History.

Barracks Street was changed to Customhouse, then back to Barracks.

And let's not forget Desire Street, from the famous Tennessee

Williams "Streetcar" play. It was christened for Desiree Montreuil, daughter of Robert Gautier Montreuil.

The swampy area in the back of town section of New Orleans was known as Marais Street. Marais is Spanish for marsh. There is also a Bayou Road, so called from all the flooding in back of town. Perdido Street was created from persons losing their way in the swamps. It means "portage of the lost." In New Orleans' early days, every street running back a dozen blocks into the swamp was a possible Perdido Street.

One of the Crescent City's most popular shopping venues is Magazine Street. Along this original route, tobacco and other goods were stored in magazins or almazons—warehouses—for export.

The Warehouse District is well known for its Julia Street, home of the Children's Museum. Legend says this route was named after landowner Julien Poydras' cook, Julia Mathew, a free woman of color. However, it could be Poydras' nickname; early maps called the street "Julie."

University Place, where Tulane Medical Center rests, was once known as Philippa, after the daughter of Governor Carondelet.

Just beneath the Highway 90 overpass heading toward the Crescent City Connection, lie streets named after the nine muses: Calliope, Clio, Erato, Thalia, Melpomene, Euterpe, Polymnia, Urania and Terpsichore.

Believe it or not, there was once a Rue de Craps, derived from the game of dice. The Rue des Bon Enfants (Good Children) is now called St. Claude. Victory Street was dubbed after General Jackson's victory at Chalmette in the Battle of New Orleans. Whodunnit fans can walk down Mystery Street when heading to JazzFest from City Park.

Now here's the best street story of all. There were plans to build a canal dividing the original French Quarter from the American section of New Orleans. The street was 171 feet wide; fifty feet were reserved for the canal. In 1852 the Orleans Navigation Company went belly up. The canal-that-never-was was legally entitled to remain a street. Merchant Judah Touro left a hefty sum in his will to beautify Canal Street. It was renamed Touro Avenue, but was changed back in 1855 for reasons unknown. Intersecting Canal Street were plans for a turning basin. Without a canal, there's no need for a basin. But there's still a Basin Street. Maybe that's where the tune *Basin Street Blues* came from.

The back side of the Quarter was originally designed for ramparts against Indian attack. The ramparts may have been in theory only but the name remains.

Okay, now it's time to hop on a streetcar and head into the American sector of the Big Easy. All aboard for Uptown!

St. Charles Avenue, our streetcar line, is so-named after the King of Spain. We're now making the circumference of Lee Circle, in honor of General Robert E. Lee and his famous monument. Until 1876, it was called Tivoli Place.

As we travel into the Garden District, we'll come across an area reserved to build a Coliseum. That never matured, but the street name did. Another cancelled construction was a Prytanee, a preparatory school derived from Prytaneum in ancient Greece. The original Prytaneum was dedicated to Hestia, the goddess of the hearth; the sacred fire: the religious and political center of the village. But New Orleans did get a fine street name out of the nixed deal: Prytania.

There's also a Market Street, after a market that was never built. Go figure.

In Uptown, boundaries of plantations gave way to Upperline and Lowerline Streets. Carrolton Street came from William Carroll, general of the militia and later a governor of Tennessee. Napoleon Avenue resulted in 1834 from the city's excitement over the diminutive French leader. Other roads were named after Napoleon's victories: Milan, Austerlitz, Marengo and Constantinople. The victory of Berlin Street was altered to General Pershing Street during World War 1.

Before we finish our street level tour, let's head back to the Quarter to do a little alley work. Either side of Saint Louis Cathedral boasts an alleyway. Pere Antoine Alley is named after a beloved Capuchin priest, Antonio de Sedella. Antonio was first sent to New Orleans in 1779 as Inquisitor. When the Spanish authorities found out, they banned him. Sedella later returned as rector of the cathedral. Antonio's wise and kind treatment of his parishioners earned him the respectful name Pere Antione…and an alley. As far as Pirate's Alley, its name sprang from Jean Lafitte and his infamous Barataria pirates. Lafitte was supposed to have met in this alley with Andrew Jackson in 1815 to plan the Battle Of New Orleans, but the alley wasn't built until the 1830's. But the name still fascinates visitors.

Whew! I'm sure I've missed several streets you may have wondered about. But I did manage to catch quite a few in my net. So next time you're wandering the streets of the Big Easy, impress your friends with your intimate knowledge of this paved history lesson. Who knows, you may even get a tour guide's tip.

# §4
# *Dis 'n Dat*

*The carousel at City Park*

# Kid Stuff

SINCE OUR SON Sean came roaring in on the scene in 1993, it's harder to get down to the Crescent City as often as we used to. So Brenda and I began to do different things, go different places, take in a whole 'nother set of sights…just to accommodate the kid.

But you know what? We adults had a whole lotta fun, too!

Now I'd never take a pre-teen down Bourbon Street, no matter what time of day it was. Way too many questions concerning those appendages in the windows. Or, "Daddy can we go see those ladies dance?" Or, "What's that mean about 'suckin' heads' on that T-shirt?" And he'd get real bored on Royal Street, peering in at all those gorgeous antiques and pricey paintings. Although the Blue Dog Gallery had him glued to the sidewalk for a while.

So we got creative.

It was Thanksgiving weekend, 2000. The Bayou Classic was in town. I'd always thought it was a golf tournament until I read about the great football rivalry between Southern University and Grambling. No wonder hotel rates went from $59 a night on Thursday to almost triple for the weekend.

We found a great rate at the Doubletree on Canal, just across from Harrah's Casino.

Sean was so proud of his first "apartment." Unfortunately, the kid wasn't allowed into Harrah's convenient, all-you-can-eat buffet, let alone their gambling facilities. Not to worry. There's always the jazz brunch at The Court of Two Sisters.

Brenda and I pigged out on everything in sight while Sean picked at his rice, mac and cheese, and a slice of King Cake (he didn't get the baby). We were all stuffed and ready for a walk to the Aquarium.

If you haven't tried out the Aquarium Of The Americas before (or lately), it's a great way to spend a few hours with a youngster. There're all kinds of photo opportunities with cockatoos, turtles, penguins, sharks, stingrays, and even an albino alligator. The tickets are reasonable, and an even better deal when you buy them in conjunction with the IMAX theatre next door and/or a Zoo Cruise up the Mississippi.

The IMAX is well worth losing yourself for an hour or so while gazing at their skyscraper size screen. We caught a show about the pyramids of Egypt with Omar Sharif. Breathtaking. And we didn't have to keep a constant eye on Sean.

By the way, the Aquarium and IMAX are both open on Thanksgiving Day, but not the Zoo Cruise.

Speaking of turkey day, not many restaurants are open Thanksgiving night, especially the familiar kid spots like Wendy's and McDonald's. Either dig into your ice chest and be creative or drop in on a neighborhood convenience store.

Looking for a unique family ride that's absolutely free? The ferry from Riverwalk to Algiers is a great way to stretch your legs while taking in a whole different view of the city.

If you ferry 'cross the Mississippi during daylight hours, be sure to take in Blaine Kern's Mardi Gras World. It's just a short walk from Algiers landing. Mardi Gras World is home to the krewe of Bacchus and all their colorful, creative floats. Drop by the "den" for an extreme closeup of Bacchasaurus, King, Queen and Baby Kong, Bacchuwhopper and all the other trappings of one of Carnival's biggest and most expressive superkrewes. Don't forget your camera.

By night, an Algiers ferry ride is a truly romantic experience with the neon-lit backdrop of the French Quarter. Remember not to stand at the front of the ferry…unless you're just itching for an unplanned wave or two.

While we're still near the Quarter, check out Musee Conti, the city's wax museum. It's at 917 Conti Street, three blocks down

Dauphine off Canal. 2 for 1 admission tickets can be found in the Good Times Guide, online, or in area magazines. Kids may not be adept to New Orleans history, but the wax figures of Napoleon in his bathtub, Andy Jackson and the Battle Of New Orleans, and a voodoo ritual are fun to view. Plus the monsters in the horror section are a great way to end the tour.

The Audubon Zoo is a no-brainer and a most excellent adventure. Just head out St. Charles Avenue towards Audubon Park and turn left at the appropriate sign. The swamp exhibit is a treat, as is the seal pool, the train ride, the reptile house and the ape area. The Zoo is a day unto itself with plenty of souvenirs to show the kids back home.

I highly recommend The Children's Museum, a two-story playhouse at 420 Julia Street in the Warehouse District. It draws kids like flypaper. The Museum features a world of interactivities from grocery shopping to puppet shows to making kid size bubbles to doing the weather on camera. Oh, and the kids will have fun, too. Free child's admission coupons are in the Good Times Guide.

The now-defunct Jazzland has morphed into Six Flags, New Orleans, spread over 140 acres, with enough rides and themes to keep a Carnival prince or princess enthralled. Head out I-10 towards Slidell and take exit 246A where I-10 and I-510 intersect. Some of the best roller coasters in the south await you. Admission is pricey, but discount tickets are in abundance at local retailers and restaurants.

If you have the time and want to get really creative, check out one of the swamp tours. Several services (with decent discounts) can be spotted in the Good Times Guide plus local tabloids and tourist magazines. There's no better place to get up close and personal with an alligator or hear the cry of a nutria in its natural habitat.

Parents, if you thought Jazzfest was just for grownups, think again. Amid all the fabulous music, tempting food, and oppressive heat is a kids section that features an interactive area for children. One tent gives them a creative outlet to make Mardi Gras masks, In an outside area, they can add their own personal building to the cardboard city in progress. And underneath the kids music tent, they can join in a fais do do. An excited Sean was called up on stage to play tambourine with Terrance Simean and his Cajun band.

Trade off the kids, catch an act you want to see, then give mom or dad a break and do some Jazzfest kidstuff yourself. Tickets for the little ones are only a few bucks, too.

One of the most glorious and glowing fantasies to widen anyone's eyes is the Celebration In The Oaks. Beginning the Friday after Thanksgiving and running through New Year's, this mammoth display of City Park lights is an annual Big Easy family tradition.

Arrive early and line up for the driving tour. Or better yet, park nearby and stroll through the forest of lights. Miniature trains run through the park, continuously crammed with wide-eyed stargazers. Area schools decorate dozens of Christmas trees with their own special theme. For the littler ones, Storyland offers pint-sized walk-throughs sure to please. And don't forget, City Park has one of the country's oldest carousels lit up like a Christmas tree and ripe for riding. Plus tacked on to this twinkling spectacle is a large section filled with fair rides. Pay one price and ride the roller coaster, ferris wheel, bumper cars and many more as much as you like.

The Celebration In The Oaks is a surefire way to put you in the holiday spirit, N'awlins style.

So no matter what time of the year you're looking for Big Easy entertainment fit for a little prince or princess, New Orleans has platters full. Don't try to do it all in one trip. Make the fun last and grow more interesting each time you acquaint your kids with one of America's most interesting cities.

# Uptown Rulers

*(This article ran in the* Planet Weekly, *Jackson, Mississippi, Sept. 20, 2000)*

GOOD EVENING, planet Earth. Would you please welcome the heart and soul of New Orleans: the mighty, mighty Neville Brothers!

They're called Uptown Rulers from New Orleans' Thirteenth Ward, Valence Street, home of the Wild Tchoupitoulas Mardi Gras Indians.

Four separate entities, as distinct as the music they make. But when the brothers Neville unite on stage, they crank up a Family Groove like no other quartet on the planet.

Multiple award-winning biographer David Ritz (compiler of the musical lives of Ray Charles, Marvin Gaye and Aretha Franklin) captures the essence, soul and *Uptown Funk of The Brothers* (Little Brown, $24). Years of interviews, culminated in chronological breakdowns and separate but equal voices, make for dead-on, if not harrowing, stories.

"Trade places with the Neville Brothers, see if you can survive," is a lyric plucked from "The Dealer." As you sink ever further into this toxic gumbo of racism, drugs, crime and punishment, marriage and divorce, personal wars, life and death—you quickly realize: if it wasn't for their music, the Nevilles would be long extinct.

Ritz introduces us to big brother Art, aka Papa Funk: a sci-fi freak who loves to tinker, whose lead vocal on the Hawkettes' "Mardi Gras Mambo" made it a carnival tradition since 1954. He's The

Meters' leader, who toured with The Rolling Stones and set Uptown Funk in motion.

Then came Charles, who loved the ladies as much as his sax. Well-read, from Eastern mysticism to Western lit. Manacled to smack for 29 years. A five year jolt in Angola for two joints. Charlie's tenacity led to Unity and Diversity.

Next up: brother Aaron, big man with the voice of an angel. From "Tell It Like It Is" in the Sixties to Nineties duets with Linda Ronstadt, Aaron's addictions and jail time paved his path to spiritual healing.

Finally, the angry baby of the bunch: Cyril. Growing up in awe of his older brothers, this Uptown Allstar cultivated a lifetime of rage stemming from racism, bad producers and worse contracts, and the drugs that fueled his fires.

"The Brothers" is a musical history lesson with a stellar cast. Enter the Sixties recording studios of Cosimo Matassa. Jam with Allen Touissant, Harold Batiste, Ray Charles, B.B. King and Fats Domino. Chant "Hey Pockey A-way" with the brothers' uncle, Big Chief Jolly and his band of Mardi Gras Indians. Cook with the Meters and the McCartneys aboard the Queen Mary.

Respect Mommee Neville's dying wish: "Keep them boys together."

Get down in Dallas, 1977, where, after decades of playing and straying, the Neville Brothers became a family again.

The brothers have recorded 14 albums together and have sold over 10 million. They've kicked their habits, toured with the Grateful Dead, won Grammys and gained independence with their own bands. Hooking up with pros like Bill Graham, Bette Midler and Linda Ronstadt gave the Nevilles the respect, the contracts and the following they so richly deserved.

"The Brothers" combines four bad-ass rides on even badder streets. But a sense of Family and Spirituality makes coming home all the sweeter.

# WWOZ
## A Musical Tapestry

MOST VISITORS to the Big Easy end up carting home a souvenir or two to keep the memories fresh. Beignet mix or ground coffee from the Café du Monde is always a given. Perhaps several pralines from Aunt Sally's on Decatur. It's easy to find a brass mask or T-shirt from the numerous shops near the riverfront and on Bourbon Street. Or the taste connoisseur might even tote home a muffuletto from Central Grocery.

But the best New Orleans souvenir is music. And aside from the usual CD, cassette and vinyl offerings throughout the Big Easy, the most righteous source for those Crescent City sounds is as close as your computer.

Picture yourself, sitting in your dull, drab office space, pulling out your *New Orleans Good Times Guide* or surfing the net planning your next Sin City escape. You need inspiration. You need good music and real people who love the city just as much as you do to inspire you.

Just turn on your trusty computer and follow the Purple, Gold and Green brick road to Oz.

One of the nicest things that ever happened inside my tiny working quarters was the discovery of wwoz.org. A New York friend (who also has a weekend residence in the Garden District—SEE *Kindred Spirits*) e-mailed me about clicking on their web broadcast and catching the morning Traditional Jazz show on WWOZ.

Oh, my, could such a thing be possible? Could I actually pick up this station I so lovingly tune to whenever I'm in the Big Easy? I immediately followed suit. In a matter of moments, the lovely strains of vintage jazz began to mellow me out, to fill my senses and the room I call home-away-from-home. So now people passing my door might see me doing a second line around my desk with a serious N'awlins buzz going on.

Whenever I'm nearing the Birthplace of Jazz, somewhere past Hammond, Louisiana, on I-55 South, I turn my dial to 90.7 FM. That's the true sounds of New Orleans, the one and only Oz.

This public radio station had its humble beginnings in 1976, the brainchild of transplanted Texan Jerry Brock and his brother. The Nora Blatch Educational Foundation was organized that same year and was the original owner of WWOZ. "It was our idea to dedicate the station to unrecognized women in broadcasting and to further that history and culture," wrote Jerry in a September 2002 *Offbeat* Magazine commentary. "Nora Blatch is possibly the most important early woman inventor in broadcast history."

In 1986, the license to WWOZ was sold by the Nora Blatch Educational Foundation to The New Orleans Jazz & Heritage Foundation, the folks who bring you Jazz Fest. The Oz offices are currently on St. Phillip Street in the historic Treme neighborhood near Armstrong Park. But thanks to a capital campaign, all that's about to change. Wwoz is partnering with the National Park Service in the New Orleans Jazz Historical Park, to build in Armstrong Park. The 6,000 square foot building will house sound and recording studios, space for visitors, volunteers and staff, plus a satellite uplink for national broadcasts. The Jazz and Heritage Foundation has already committed $300,000 to the project.

Over the years, Oz has striven to uphold the mantle of the past as far as vintage New Orleans music is concerned. But it's also paved the way for new artists and styles to reach its listening audience. All of the Oz DJ's are volunteers, and what a warehouse of musical knowledge and sounds each possesses.

My favorite listening time is from 9-11 AM weekdays. Trad Jazz, as they call it. Each day a different DJ hosts. Tom Saunders is Monday, Don & Milly Vappie are on Tuesdays, Tom Morgan plays Wednesdays and Bob French hosts "French Cooking" on Fridays. Listening to these jazz pros (who also play around the city) is like having your own personal historian holding a "play and tell" session; laid back—Big Easy style, and what a vintage collection of hard to find albums. There's even a hot line where you can call the DJ live and ask where the heck they found that jazzy tune you're hearing.

WWOZ airs 24/7, featuring Jazz, Blues, R&B, Brass Bands, Zydeco, Swing, Irish, Latin, Brazilian, Cajun, Gospel and Bluegrass. Did I forget to mention The Kitchen Sink?

Let's head back over to the web site. Visit the Swamp Shop and order an Oz T-shirt, cap or prayer candle. Click on Back Playlists to see what you've missed. Become a loyal supporter during Oz's annual fund drive. Find out the second line schedule by checking out the Backstreet Cultural Museum site. Peek in on Jazz Fest and event listings.

Find out these cool WWOZ facts: its regular local listening audience numbers over 50,000; annual listener support is $450,000; audio streaming began in 1995 with over a million hits per month. Oz was voted Best Jazz Station Of The Year in the U.S. in 2000 and 2001 by the *Gann Report*; and the Best Radio Station in 2000 by both *Gambit Weekly* and *Offbeat* Magazine.

Surf great links like The Louisiana Music Factory at 201 Decatur Street. One of its original owners? Some Texan named Jerry Brock. Remember him? The guy who helped start all this great radio in the Crescent City? Brock was also instrumental in producing and introducing The Rebirth Brass Band to the world (SEE *Braggin' In Brass*).

It's fascinating how music seems to be woven together into the Big Easy tapestry.

The WWOZ web site says it best: "New Orleans has a truly unique place in the history of music and WWOZ is on a mission to share New Orleans' special heritage with the world." Tune in or log on and take this most precious of Big Easy souvenirs home with you.

*Author Julie Smith signs at Lemuria, Jackson, Mississippi*

## *Write Where You Live*

THE BIG EASY lends itself to some of the most entertaining tales, both real and imagined, ever produced in the South. As in its neighboring state of Mississippi, writers live in or near the area that inspires them. The late Walker Percey, whose bayou-laced journeys often included New Orleans, stayed just across Lake Pontchartrain in the quaint village of Covington. Frances Parkenson Keyes, the *Crescent Carnival* author revered in the 1930's, is honored through her home on lower Chartres Street. Beloved war historian Stephen Ambrose was a professor at Tulane before his death in 2002. The late Lloyd Vogt offered both words and sketches in *New Orleans Houses, New Orleans Buildings,* and *Historic Buildings Of The French Quarter.* Ellen Gilchrist, creator of her famed Rhoda character and New Orleans-themed stories and novels, kept a residence in the Big Easy for a number of years.

And of course, there's those two gentlemen who define southern writing, and even have annual Crescent City-based festivals held in their respective honor: William Faulkner and Tennessee Williams.

Many of today's New Orleans writers are celebrated, award-winners and bestsellers. They reside throughout the city, be it Uptown, Downtown, Mid-City or in the Quarter. Quite often, the first Crescent City author a visitor might think of is Anne Rice. After all, Rice's New Orleans settings are paramount toward the romantic and gothic doorways her characters pass through. Anne's books have brought tourists in droves to view her Garden District house, roam on vampire walking tours, even to masquerade and attend a Coven Party or two. Vampfans also need food and lodging. Anne Rice has been very good for New Orleans' economy.

Pulitzer winner Richard Ford, known for his *Independence Day* and *The Sportswriter* dwells somewhere in the Garden District. Mystery author Julie Smith, creator of the Skip Langdon and Baroness Pontalba series, keeps a place in the Faubourg Marigny. As far as authenticity, Julie's one of the best Big Easy tour guides going. Tony Dunbar is another respected Crescent City mystery scribe. His wife Mary runs Beaucoup Books on Magazine Street in Uptown. Guess Tony's a natural for her booksignings.

Horror writer Poppy Z. Brite lives in a quiet Uptown home. Andre Codrescu, author of *The Blood Countess*, resides in nearby Baton Rouge. The haunting prose of John Ed Bradley is tapped from his home in Sin City. Official biographer of Jimmy Carter and Frank Kerouac as well as a collaborator on *The Mississippi River* with Stephen Ambrose, Doug Brinkley is another proud New Orleanian. Robert Florence, author of *New Orleans Cemeteries*, has his own local tour company.

Sheila Bosworth, author of *Slow Poison* and *Almost Innocent*, can often be seen at local booksignings. The mother/daughter team of Kerri and Cynthia McCafferty have jointly and separately produced some of New Orleans' finest coffee table books, including *The Majesty of St. Charles Avenue* and *Obituary Cocktail*. James Colbert, the man behind the Skinny Man mysteries, lives in the Quarter.

New Orleanian Henri Schindler has brought us the beauty of Mardi Gras past through his fascinating pictorial books. Mr. Mardi Gras, Arthur Hardy, the man behind the annual *Carnival Guide*, lives Uptown. David Speilman, the cameraman of *Southern Writers*, a splendid book of author photos and bios, is proud to call New Orleans home. Don't forget the delightful children's books *Epossumondus* and *Who's That Trippin' Over My Bridge* by local favorite Coleen Salley.

No doubt I've overlooked dozens of Big Easy scribes. For a more comprehensive view of the rich heritage of Crescent City authors, check out *The Book Lover's Guide To New Orleans* by the *Times-Picayune*'s chief book reviewer Susan Larson. Now there's a lady who knows her writers!

There are two literary festivals that celebrate the rich literary heritage of New Orleans; one in Winter, the other in Spring.

Words & Music is a five day "literary feast" held the first weekend of December at the Hotel Monteleone, 200 Royal Street. The literary focus is called Perfect Word; there's associated food and wine events featuring music. That pretty much brings the whole gamut of New Orleans' best features together.

Words & Music's faculty includes nominees and winners of the Pulitzer, Edgar, Steinbeck Prize, the National and American Book Awards, and others. Authors of literary and commercial fiction, best-selling non-fiction, history, bio's, memoirs, journalism, coffee table and cookbooks are all assembled.

The event is billed as "five days of enlightenment and entertainment with 125 well-known authors, editors, agents and entertainers." Round table discussions, original dramas, and master classes are incorporated into the mix. New and developing writers can meet and consult one-on-one with publishing executives, editors and agents.

Tuition—including all round table discussions, advance manuscript critiques and consultations—is $300. Scholarships are available for students of accredited creative writing programs outside of Louisiana. Daily and five-day rates for those who just want to watch is considerably lower.

Words & Music is sponsored by the Pirate's Alley Faulkner Society. For years, the event was known as the Faulkner Conference. The new moniker was unveiled in 1997 during the 100th anniversary of William Faulkner's birth. The Pirate's Alley Faulkner Society is "a non-profit literary and educational organization devoted to the preservation of the story telling traditions of our region and providing realistic assistance to developing authors and other artists." Check them out at WORDS&MUSIC.COM.

In late March, the Tennessee Williams/New Orleans Literary Festival takes center stage, quite literally. Headquartered at Le Petit Theatre du Vieux Carre, 616 St. Peter Street, the five-day Tennessee Williams Fest features master classes for writers and readers with literary stars and publishing pros. Over two dozen panel discussions, celebrity interviews and beaucoups of Williams-themed theatre herald spring in the Big Easy. Master classes and panel topics range from Southern humor, screenwriting and French quarter fiction to mystery and sci-fi and memories of Williams.

Tennessee Sips, the annual wine tasting party, is always a sellout; intoxicating comparisons are made between wines and Mr. Williams' characters. Auntie Pasto and her Southern Kin, a discussion on Italian and Southern cooking, is, likewise, well attended. A one-act play competition, poetry slam, lectures, literary walking tours, musical performances and a book fair round out the Tennessee Williams/New Orleans Literary Festival.

And lastly, "but definitely loudest," is the stellar closing event: the Stanley and Stella shouting contest. Contestants line up in Jackson Square around 4:30 Sunday afternoon to test their vocal skills in the famous scene from *A Streetcar Named Desire*. At 5:30, the finals commence. This is a shouting match not to be missed.

Past festival stars include Patricia Neal, Alec Baldwin, Eli Wallach, Anne Jackson, Edward Albee, Rex Reed and Williams' "baby" brother Dakin.

Celebrating its seventeenth year in 2003, fan influx has caused the Tennessee Williams Festival to outgrow its original site. Corresponding events are held at the Cabildo, the Historic New Orleans Collection, the Hotel Monteleone, Muriel's Jackson Square Restaurant, Brennan's, O'Flaherty's Irish Channel Pub, the Palm Court Jazz Café, and the Contemporary Arts Center. The festival is overseen by a volunteer board of directors: teachers, writers, book-sellers, city government personnel, corporate reps, and TV consultants.

Tickets to master classes are $35 each or $375 for the complete series. Theatre seats and other events can be secured through Ticketweb at 1-800-965-4827 or on-line through the festival web site: TENNESSEEWILLIAMS.NET.

New Orleans is perhaps the most literary city on the planet, thanks to its rich talent pool of citizenry and two of the best writers conferences anywhere.

## Call For Distress

No doubt about it, New Orleans spawns some of the best tales ever told. When one conjures thoughts of a Sin City story, visions usually swerve dead-on into the path of Mardi Gras. After all, that's when things are at their wickedest, their most ribald and chancy. Gaudy, baudy and naughty: that's New Orleans. Breasts flashing almost every block of Bourbon Street; a jester-clad couple doing the nasty on a second floor balcony above the cheers of enthralled onlookers; epic phalluses protruding from costumed revelers on rollerskates; a silver spraypainted street person threatening the populace with a loaded banana. Well, maybe not, but you get the picture.

My favorite Big Easy story isn't strewn with litter or exposed body parts. No drunk frat boys regurgitating in Pirate's Alley or coercing enhanced damsels for mega-beads.

But it's still a good 'un, anyway.

Keith Wehmeier, my ex-cop cohort who shared bits of his life in *Volume One*, never tires from fantastic Crescent City episodes. Being one of New Orleans' finest for fifteen years can produce a treasure trove of titular tales. Most you can't share.

A few years ago, Keith developed diabetes. The energy depletion was too much to remain on the force. So he retired.

Keith became a tour guide much to his (and wife Deb's) relief. When it rains or a group gets cancelled, he takes in a movie. One Friday afternoon while I was visiting, Keith talked me into catching

*Undercover Brother*, which I never would've seen on my own. Word of mouth works everytime. Plus the Elmwood Cinema in Metairie is a masterpiece in controlled chaos.

*Undercover Brother* was everything Keith had predicted, except for the extremely noisy black chicks sitting to my left. When I asked the raucous duo to keep it down, the largest lady sitting mere inches from my person glared at me and uttered, "Who you talkin' to?!"

I chose to laugh as loudly as I could for the remainder of the flick in lieu of losing badly in a race war I'd never meant to start.

We were heading home; I'm licking my movie patron wounds while Keith trolls the finer points of New Orleans life. Out of the blue, this former narcotics officer begins recounting the time they had a hostage situation over at one of the area TV stations.

"What?" I shouted. "When?"

He's got me now. The Blazer swerves past a pedestrian as we cross Earnhart to Broad. Keith reverts to tourist guide mode, a la Dragnet's Joe Friday.

"It was around 1986. I was working the Sixth Precinct at the time," he recalls. "Overnight shift; 11-7. This call comes in around 12:30 AM; middle of the night. Some guy's watching an old episode of Rowan and Martin's *Laugh-In* on WVUE, channel 8."

While the viewer chuckles over Goldie Hawn dancing in a bikini and Artie Johnson muttering, "Very eeenteresting," a crawling banner appears at the bottom of the screen: "Help! I'm being held captive in the control room."

"So the precinct house gets the call," Keith says. "The guy's understandably upset. By the time we arrive, it's a legitimate call for distress."

Several cop cars pull up to WVUE. The officers carefully force their way into the building. The men in blue troll the hallways, hearts pounding at the sinister quiet. They slip into the master control room, guns drawn, expecting crazed maniacs holding wounded and/or dying employees on the floor, a hand-held remote set for instant destruction.

They're met by two perplexed overnight operators.

No guns. No hostage situation. Just Rowan and Martin's *Laugh-In*. The cry for help was part of an "in-show" prank recorded over twenty years earlier. I'm sure the producers never expected their time capsule to have such an impact on NOPD. Or the hapless master control operators at WVUE.

"They nearly peed their pants," laughs Keith.

Imagine, a quiet Friday night at a lonely TV station, getting your kicks from Dan Rowan and Dick Martin, and suddenly, there's four or five guns in your face.

I shudder to think how things might be in today's terrorist-laden terrain.

Sometimes Truth is stranger than...*Laugh-In*!

*Suspense novelist John Connolly and the author*

# Time Well Spent

*Friday, April 11, 3:00 PM*

JUST STEPPED OFF the streetcar at Washington and St. Charles. Had to wait twenty minutes for it to show up. I could've stayed back on Bourbon Street with all those jazz bands.

So many stops since Canal Street; thought we'd never make it here. I'm hot from my long-sleeve navy blue T-shirt; better roll up the sleeves. Feeling a bit sluggish from all the beer and food last night and today, all the walking since 10:00 this morning. Tired, but elated. So much crammed into such a short time. Time well spent.

I'm ambling towards The Rink on the corner of Prytania. Lafayette Cemetery Nº 1 looms on the right, Commander's Palace is on the left. I tend to forget these landmarks; I see them so much. Traffic is light, trees are in bloom, weather is perfect.

A voice in the back of my head keeps repeating the same phrase: "You're leaving paradise."

My silver Mitsubishi Eclipse awaits, dust-covered and bedecked with smashed bugs. It'll be hot as hell inside.

I climb the steps of The Rink to get a few quick hugs and handshakes from my compatriots; the friends I spent so much time with yesterday.

I start up the engine, pop in my new CD and head back to St. Charles, knowing it's gonna be a long three hours, including stop-and-go traffic on I-10, before I can settle down for an anniversary dinner back home, replete with mudbugs, boiled shrimp, fried catfish, and oysters on the halfshell. Quite an incentive.

"You're leaving paradise," the voice whispers again. "Yeah, I know," I think to myself. "But hasn't it been great?"

### 23 Hours Earlier

What a quick trip! Those three hours just flew by. Thoughts of being manacled to the camera at work are long gone; client calls will have to wait. I can write those commercials next week. Hell, I'm in the Garden District at 4:06 PM on a gorgeous Thursday afternoon. One of my favorite writers is signing in about an hour, and I've got nothing to do but catch up with friends and maybe take a walk down the avenue on this perfect Spring day.

A parking place awaits me right in front of the Rink. Always a good sign.

I walk through the double doors, books and camera in tow. Ted stands at the top of the stairs, outside the Garden District Book Shop. "You seen Connolly?" he asks. "He'll probably be late like last time."

Shelves of books in tight quarters seem to wink as I pass. Amy's behind the counter. "I've got something for you," she smiles, and hands me her corrections on the manuscript for *Mo' Dreamin'*. Soon as I finish tweaking it on computer, I'll be able to get the new volume to Jason, my designer.

"So you think it'll fly?" I ask. "Oh, yeah," Amy replies. "I like it." A good sign. Amy doesn't pull any punches.

Deb chats with a customer near the children's section. She beams a hello and asks, "Do you need a key to the house?" "Nope," I say, "I'll be riding with you tonight."

I page my New York buddy John on the store's phone. He should be in town for the weekend, working as a volunteer for the French Quarter Festival. No call back.

Author John Connolly's signing table is in front of the store entrance. Wine is being set out along with crackers, cheese and other munchies. Wine connoisseur Steve, a store regular, gives his blessing on the bottles. If Steve likes it, it's gotta be good.

Book shop owner Britton Trice is busy packing books for an evening signing at someone's home in the French Quarter. He'll catch up with us as the evening progresses. I try a cup of the white wine. Steve was right. I try another. Mmm…

Welcome back to the Big Easy, JC!

*5:20 PM*

The featured author's late. Ted heard John Connolly was antiquarian book shopping in the Quarter. I walk up a small flight of stairs to The Anne Rice Collection. My friend Sue, whom I'd hoped to see, isn't working here anymore. A couple weeks back, Sue was asked to be Anne Rice's "special personal assistant." Anne had surgery recently; there was a big article in the *Times-Picayune* about it on Wednesday, someone says. "Hmmm," I think. "I'll have to change the ending to Suzie Q's essay."

I find long-time Rice fan and employee Michael behind the sales desk. A paper-sized note taped to the wall says the store is closing in a week. "This is it for me," Michael sighs. He's going back into real estate full-time. It's nice to see him happy again. Well, as happy as Michael will ever allow himself to be.

We exchange spoilers on the final five episodes of *Buffy The Vampire Slayer*. I buy a small Dracula pendant. It's half price, and so appropriate. I'm directing the vampire play this Halloween.

I'm still checking out discounted jewelry when I notice a small man in black enter The Rink. Strains of an Irish accent. Finally, I get to meet the guy whose books I've been reviewing for four years, the man who's captivated the world with his wickedly sinister crime novels, *Every Dead Thing*, *Dark Hollow*, *The Killing Kind*, and *The White Road*.

John Connolly's engaged in conversation as I approach. "Where's the reviewer from the *Clarion-Ledger*?" he asks, his back to me. "Here!" I reply, like a shy schoolboy.

John turns and grins. "You up for that pint I owe you tonight?" he says. "You bet," I smile, and we shake hands.

*7:05 PM*

Steeped in wine and running on smiles, John Connolly's signing has been a fun gathering. He's attracted several admirers, who share my delight in fawning over the author. Ted's roommate Cindy dropped by to get her book signed. She was decked out in an eye-catching tux top and shorts. Cindy was headed to the Quarter to be the photo girl at Pat O'Brien's; part of her unique job. I snapped off numerous shots myself, including one of John and Deb, who has a modest crush on the Irishman. "Isn't he the nicest guy," she beams.

Connolly even bought a copy of *Big Easy Dreamin'*. I was so honored to sign it for him.

The store's closing, but the adventure continues. "Where're we gonna eat," Deb inquires. Someone suggests Joey K's, a neighborhood restaurant a few blocks away on Seventh Street. "Sounds good to me," Connolly replies. "As long as they serve alcohol."

I leave my vehicle at the store and hitch a ride with Deb in her white Blazer.

**9:30 PM**

A thought passes through me in the back room of Joey K's, surrounded by friends, old and new, stuffed to the gills with Veal Parmesan, spaghetti, and a tankard of Abita Amber: "I've been included in one of the nicest literary encounters I've attended in a long while. I'm sitting next to one of my favorite authors. I'm in New Orleans. Tomorrow's French Quarter Fest. If this isn't a heavenly scenario, I don't know what is."

Connolly is a most well-read individual, besides being an ardent soccer fan. And boy, can he hold his pints. John has an early flight the next morning to Birmingham; needs to be up by 5:45, at the airport by 7:00.

"Which bar do we go to, Ted," Amy wonders. "Why ask me," inquires Ted. "You know all the right ones," someone adds.

We remain Uptown and head over to The Columns Hotel on St. Charles. Couldn't have picked a nicer place. Our group sat at a wrought iron table on the beautiful front porch, watching streetcars cross in both directions. A small black kitty jumped up in my lap and nestled in for the duration. Reminded me of my old grey cat Ash, who used to perch on my chest in the recliner. (I didn't realize how much I missed him.)

The weather began to dip into the low 60's. I was a bit chilled with only a T-shirt and jeans, but didn't give it much thought. The beer ran freely and the chatter was non-stop. Britton joined us later and congratulated his guest on a successful signing.

*Midnight*

The last eight hours have been marvelous. John Connolly gave me a hearty handshake and headed off to the Quarter where he's staying. I'm taking a chance and leaving my car at the store. Deb's driving me to her place where the guest bed's turned down. Visions of French Quarter Fest play in my head as I quickly drift into sleep.

*4:15 AM*

Thank God for Alka-Seltzer!

*9:00 AM*

Completely missed Deb's husband Keith. He'd already left by 8:00 AM to conduct a French Quarter tour before I stumbled out for breakfast. I'm greeted by aging beagles Watson and Mr. Peabody. They wonder why I don't have time to toss them a ball. Deb has to head out early to pick up an altar cloth at the cleaners for her church. I wolf down a croissant and milk, and we're on our way.

Our Lady Of Good Counsel, on the corner of Louisiana and Chestnut, is gorgeous in its antiquity and inspiring stained glass. We huddle at the altar, drape the cloth, and gaze at the humbling surroundings, built in 1878. I feel Our Lady glimpsing down on us, a couple days shy of Palm Sunday. No wonder Deb likes coming here so much.

My car's still intact in front of the Rink. I wait a few minutes for the St. Charles streetcar, then it's down to the Quarter.

*11:00 AM*

Been strolling for about an hour on this most excellent day. Went by the Louisiana Music Factory, where I purchased a CD I'd read about in *Offbeat* Magazine. "Straight From The Sixth Ward" is a collection of some of that neighborhood's best brass bands, including The Rebirth, The New Birth, The Treme, and the Sixth Ward Allstars. One listen was all it took.

Checked out a few bookstores on my way to Jackson Square. The crowds are really getting thick. I remember, years ago, no one even knew about The French Quarter Fest (FQF). Now, it's huge, twenty years strong.

My timing is impeccable. A few moments before the gates open for the World's Largest Jazz Brunch inside Jackson Square, I hear an approaching parade. There they come, down Rue St. Ann, marchers with gaily-adorned umbrellas, preceding a brass band. The bystanders are all whipped up, cheering and clapping. The official FQF marchers head through the gates toward the festival's heaping helpings of food, beer, water and T-shirts. The throng follows suit.

A few moments after opening remarks by the mayor and other dignitaries, Pete Fountain begins to play on the Southern Comfort stage in this "made to order" weather. I grabbed a Miller draft and ordered up a bowl of seafood pasta from the Begue's Restaurant tent. What will I eat next?

**2:15 PM**

Bruce O'Neil & His Hard Working Jazz Band are tearin' it up on the 200 block of Bourbon Street at Legends Park. An elderly lady with an umbrella weaves in front of the band, beckoning fans to come out and dance. A little girl steps up, grabs the woman's bumbershoot, and begins strutting. The group cheers. A few hours earlier, the Pete Fountain statue was dedicated here. Pete stands just to the right of Al Hirt's image.

I've caught one trad-jazz band per block since the 700 block of Bourbon. There's five stages on this one street alone; over fourteen stages throughout the Quarter.

So many wonderful sights, sounds, smells and tastes have opened up to me over the last three hours. The Woldenberg Riverfront Park held a bevy of food tents and several music stages. The Mighty Mississippi moves boats of every size and dimension through its muddy current. Families and individuals lay on blankets, gorge on succulent tastes, and soak up the atmosphere. Right here, right now, this is the perfect time to be in New Orleans. As trumpeter Kermit Ruffins would say, "Yes, indeeed!"

I really hate to do this, but I gotta head back to Canal Street and wait for the streetcar for Uptown. It's time to go home.

But I plan to carry this Big Easy feeling all the way back with me. Let it spread throughout the confines of Sal & Phil's Restaurant in Ridgeland, where I'll be dining on the eve of mine and Brenda's 23$^{rd}$ anniversary. Let it nurture me the following week, when I'm busy at work.

Let it remind me that paradise is only a three hour drive away.

# That Big Easy Feeling

WHEN I WAS PROMOTING my first volume of New Orleans essays, Jack Sweitzer of ETV's *Open Air* asked me at what point during a journey down to the Crescent City did I begin to feel that freeing effect the area gave me. I knew right away.

"As soon as I cross the state line," I beamed.

I've often wondered if it was just the recently paved roads Louisiana provides to give you a welcome-mat feeling to the state. Although my tires appreciate the fresh asphalt, I realize the sensation is more akin to spiritual than a lack of potholes.

Something clicks in my subconscious; the real me begins to emerge. I know that within a ninety minute span, I'll be in the land of dreamy dreams, the place that welcomes my soul rather than just my credit card. New Orleans and vicinity seems to ascertain my needs and desires like a lover.

Jack asked my favorite locale in the Big Easy. Another no-hesitancy answer: the steps leading down to the river at the Moonwalk. They could sprinkle my ashes here. Above all other locales in New Orleans (even the dripping oaks on St. Charles), a solitary view of a passing tanker, the distant car lights crossing over the bridge into Algiers, the ferry sloshing over to unload its cargo, a lone sax player standing sentinel…and just the river itself: the calm, serene waters that have seen so much history unfold…these are the simple pleasures that surround me with an unquenchable joy and reverence for my city.

I could sit here forever.

My buddy Bert has never felt so charged as when he accompanies me to New Orleans. We've come a long way from getting rained on at a Mardi Gras parade a few years back. Bert has discovered a new-found confidence the Big Easy offers. "I'm away from my job, all the expected pressures that home demands," Bert says.

In New Orleans, Bert can create a lavish latex vampire face, shove in some fangs, pull on a black leather trenchcoat and become his role-playing alter ego Spike from *Buffy The Vampire Slayer*. He can meet lady vamps at an Anne Rice Halloween party, become a seductive villain and lure them into some darkened dressing room.

"Down here I'm me," Bert exclaims. "New Orleans lets you break free of the restrictions other people put upon you. It gives you permission to be your true self."

Peter Meyers, a hometown boy now living in Jackson, Mississippi, drives down as often as possible. "It's the people," he says. "Lifelong friends. I like to look at New Orleans as my watering hole. I get a good soak, then I can go on."

Peter enjoys riding up and down St. Charles Avenue where he grew up, seeing Tulane, Loyola and Audubon Park. "It's my life, visually," Peter says. "I carry it with me, then come down and renew."

My pal Wayni Terrell puts it most eloquently. "The city has sounds and smells that provoke feelings to permeate your soul," the Canton, Mississippi artist drawls. "The smell of the concrete on Rue Royal after a brief, summer rain…hot jazz spilling from every little corner…the night time sounds of holiday tourists on Rue Chartres the week before Christmas.

"But my favorite feeling is sitting in a courtyard in the early, early morning, before dawn. If you sit very still, you can almost catch that sweet sound of Satchmo's trumpet, Sweet Emma's piano, Big Jim's trombone…and smell the combination of that music, the emotions driving it, and the soft rain that falls on almost empty streets…and you know you're home."

Thanks for the quote, sweetie. Maybe you should have written this book.

I've watched uptight mid-western tourists dance a jig on Bourbon Street with wild abandon, knowing they'd never do this back home. I've felt the unbridled joy of tens of thousands in a Mardi Gras throng; if only you could bottle that kind of euphoria. I've admired a couple walking hand in hand in Jackson Square at twilight: she, in a soft pastel sundress, her partner in jeans and a T-shirt. Like Stella and Stanley Kowalski in *A Streetcar Named Desire*. Gaslights begin to flicker, sensuality is heady all around them.

Enjoy your evening, folks, I remark to myself. The town's ripe for plucking.

New Orleans is an empathic city. It senses your burdens, then drapes them with a big quilt of kindness; a valet that constantly follows you around to make sure you're taken care of, no tip necessary.

I get that Big Easy feeling whenever I listen to traditional jazz, especially Louis Armstrong. Today's modern equivalent to Satchmo, trumpeter Kermit Ruffins, once remarked that if God had a voice, he would surely sound like King Louis.

New Orleans is all about the music, the food, the people, and the ambiance. And it's all about the memories they cultivate, that glaze your subconscious like Carnival glitter.

Am I tempting you, urging you to start planning your next Big Easy getaway? Good. There's a lot of blues in this old world. And New Orleans is the best place to cure 'em.

Even if it's only in your mind.

# Afterword
## — Sin City Self Serve —

THE PARADE has passed. The final truck float is rolling slowly up Napoleon, eager hands in the distance poised to snatch up plush toys and beads-by-the-ton. But from where we sit, the performance is complete. The purple, gold and green curtain has fallen. Ladders are being folded. Exhausted children hang limply from their parents' shoulders. Elderly revelers in bright colors collapse their folding chairs, their sacks tightly packed with treasure.

Empty beer cans, soft drink and water bottles, fried chicken containers, and sandwich wrappers share an exotic mix with mutilated beads, broken beyond repair.

I pause to catch my breath, stretching before I rise. My bag forces the chair to topple with ten pounds of Carnival captures. We're nearly alone now, the weary participants shuffling off towards home or parked cars.

But I can almost smell the red beans and rice cooking four blocks away, can almost taste the jambalaya and deviled eggs. My mouth waters for just one bite of a Popeye's fried chicken breast.

And I can't wait to play show-and-tell with my friends camped on the front porch.

Hope you've enjoyed the parade within the pages of this book as much as I've taken pleasure in sprucing up the floats. In my research for *Mo' Dreamin'*, I've rekindled friendships, strengthened others, and opened up many new channels of information I'd only glimpsed from the surface. I feel richly rewarded for gleaning, then passing on my findings to you.

Now you won't blanch when someone casually mentions Voodoo. You might want to attend a Super Sunday afternoon with the Mardi Gras Injuns. You'll have a deeper appreciation for riverboats, social aid clubs, brass bands, and the musical and literary festivals that honor the city. You can hop aboard the City Of New Orleans for your next (or first) Mardi Gras excursion. You might grab a piece of prime real estate with a balcony. You can impress your friends with your new vast knowledge of street histories. Or stick in some fangs and pay homage at an Anne Rice coven party.

There's lots of heavenly scenarios when you go Big Easy Dreamin'. You're perfectly welcome to create a few of your own from this spicy buffet.

It's a Sin City self serve, dawlin'.

# Sources

*New Orleans Good Times Guide*
CARLMACK.COM
BARKUS.ORG
KREWEDUVIEUX.ORG
MARDIGRASINDIANS.COM
SATCHMOSUMMERFEST.ORG
CAJUNHOT.COM
Lafayette Convention and Visitors Commission
WWOZ.ORG
NOJOURNAL.COM
AMTRAK.COM
*Train* Magazine; "City Of New Orleans" article by Bob Johnson
VOODOOSHOP.COM
VOODOOMUSEUM.COM
VOODOOSPIRITUALTEMPLE.ORG
WORDS&MUSIC.ORG
Ritz, David; *The Brothers Neville*; New York; Little, Brown Publishers; 2000
Cook, Samantha; *The Rough Guide To New Orleans*; Rough Books; Penguin Press, 2002
TENNESSEEWILLIAMS.NET
Huber, Leonard, *New Orleans, A Pictorial History*, New York; Crown Publishers, 1971, Gretna, LA; Pelican Publishing Co., 1991
Chase, John Churchill; *Frenchmen, Desire, Good Children*, Robert L. Crager & Co., New Orleans, 1960; originally published in 1949
Saxon, Lyle; *Voodoo In New Orleans*; Pelican Publishing Co., New Orleans, 1983; originally published by McMillan, New York, 1946
KUSTOMKARDS.COM
MARDIGRASDIGEST.COM
Ramsland, Katherine; *Prism Of The Night*; New York, Dutton Press, 1991
NOLA.COM
*Offbeat* Magazine, July, 2002; "Dirty Dozen Brass Band...From Birthdays to Funerals and Everything in Between," Geraldine Wyckoff
*Offbeat* Magazine, September, 2002; "WWOZ: Community Radio...Or Not?" by Jerry Brock
Schedule and information flyer from the Steamboat Natchez
GET-WAXED.COM
KREWEOFMUSES.ORG
*Mardi Gras* Magazine 2003; "Girls Gone Wild" (krewe of Muses article) by Jyl Benson
REBIRTHBRASSBAND.COM
DONNASBARANDGRILL.COM
TIMESPICAYUNE.COM

## *The Author*

**JC PATTERSON** was born and raised in Vicksburg, Mississippi, and now resides in Madison, Mississippi, with his wife, son, cat, turtles and beagle Sookie. JC has had a long-term love affair with the Crescent City and finds any excuse for a weekend visit, hence the culmination of *Big Easy Dreamin'*, Volumes 1 & 2. He is a writer/producer/interviewer/voice talent at WLBT-TV3 in Jackson, Mississippi, and has appeared in dozens of TV commercials and hundreds of radio and TV voiceovers. An avid reader and freelance book critic, JC has contributed over 300 book reviews to the Jackson *Clarion-Ledger* and *Planet Weekly* newspapers. For over 20 years, JC has produced, directed, promoted and performed with numerous theatres across central Mississippi.

But nothing beats the sounds of a hot brass band, the smell (and taste) of Cajun boiled crawfish, or an early morning walk in the Vieux Carre.

# *Need Mo' Copies?*

To order *Big Easy Dreamin'* Volumes 1 and/or 2,
Send a check for $14 (each copy; includes postage) to

JC Patterson
3012 Tidewater Circle
Madison, Mississippi 39110